Pasquale Di Bello

Stampa Alternativa/Nuovi Equilibri
Collana Sconcerto
Prima Edizione Ottobre 1992

GRATEFUL DEAD

Le parole nella penna sono tante come le persone cui devo la mia "riconoscenza" per essere state qui, ad un solo passo dalle righe di questo libro e a nessuno dal mio cuore. Agli amici cari e lontani della fanzine Ripple, primi a salire dal pozzo dei sogni, particolarmente a Claudio Franco, compagno inseparabile fin dai tempi della piazzetta. Ai tanti altri trovati per strada, a quelli che mi hanno aiutato ed ora sono tra le pagine che seguono, all'amico fraterno Johnny Blasi per l'insuperabile consulenza sul San Francisco sound; Ambrogio Facchetti, Lucia Giardino e mio fratello Nicola che hanno cercato un vestito per le mie parole; Elena Piccioni per l'appassionato ed indimenticabile incoraggiamento; l'editore e Gigi Marinoni per l'infinita pazienza usatami. Con altri sono in qualche modo in debito; con la Wild Bird Records ed infine con gli amici Daniele Pelli, Antonio Arnaldo, Annalisa Onorato, Stefano Focacci, Gianni Rosati e Stefano Cellai.
Questo libro è dedicato ai miei genitori, a una stella ed ai gatti Jenny, Jack e Gabibbo sicuramente in corsa sulla pista felice.

Pasquale di Bello - Firenze, Ottobre 1992

Words in my pen are many and many as the people that I must be "grateful" for being here, just a step away from these lines and no distance from my heart. To the dear friends of the Ripple fanzine, the first that came out from the dreams pit, particularly to Claudio Franco, old buddy form the piazzetta times. To the many other that I found along the road, to the ones that helped me and now are in the following pages, to the fraternal friend Johnny Blasi for the unexcelled advice on San Francisco sound; Ambrogio Facchetti, Lucia Giardino and my brother Nicola that has looked for a new dress for my words; Elena Piccioni for the passionate and unforgettable encouragement; to the publisher and to Gigi Marinoni with boundless patience. I owe something to other people too, with Wild Bird Records and last but not least to my friends Daniele Pelli, Antonio Arnaldo, Annalisa Onorato, Stefano Focacci, Gianni Rosati and Stefano Cellai.
This book is dedicated to my parents, to a star and to the kittens Jenny, Jack and Gabibbo surely running on the happy trail.

di/by: Pasquale Di Bello
Copertina/Cover: Piermario Ciani
Artwork pag. 1/95: Matteo Guarnaccia, skeleton pag. 70: Gianluca Lerici
Computer graphic pag. 33/67/90: Piermario Ciani
Composizione/Typesetting: Watermelon - Milano
Fotolito/Photolitos: Graphos - Pero (Mi)
Stampa/Printing: Union Printing Viterbo

CAN YOU PASS THE ACID TEST?

Quando nel 1850 la California diventa il 31°
stato dell'Unione, la memoria storica dell'America perde definitivamente l'idea e il mito della
"frontiera". Due oceani per confini ed
un'immensità di terre senza recinti. Forse per
destino o per vocazione, in California il sogno
americano é tentato ad andare "oltre", un passo
più in là della frontiera e della porta dell'ordinario. Un filo invisibile lega la nostra storia a
questo destino. Il luogo dell'azione é San
Francisco, fiore sbocciato sull'oceano, qui
comincia e prende rima la ballata del "morto
riconoscente", tutto in un passato talmente
prossimo nel cuore da sembrare oggi.
Mentre buona parte dell'America dorme il sogno
del benessere post-bellico, un'altra si scuote e
si sveglia, e col vento negli occhi parte per una
nuova corsa all'oro. Il "Rinascimento" che
sboccia a San Francisco nei primi anni '60 trova
il suo humus culturale nel circuito beat del
decennio precedente.
Era da queste parti che avevano trovato una
patria ideale gente come Kerouac, Burroughs,
Ginsberg, Corso e tanti altri figli del sole meridiano. North Beach all'epoca era il quartier
generale dei Beatniks, così come il City Light
Bookstore di Lawrence Ferlinghetti era meta del
nuovo circuito letterario.
A trafiggere il cielo sereno erano arrivate anche
le visioni del grande padre psichedelico, Aldous
Huxley. E' il 1954 quando il vecchio filosofo e
letterato pubblica *Le Porte della Percezione*,
parabola ante litteram del misticismo chimico.
E' in questo clima che sul finire del 1959, al
Veterans Hospital di Menlo Park cominciano una
serie di esperimenti sugli effetti delle sostanze
allucinogene.
L'occasione era data da un programma di
ricerca governativo sulla schizofrenia e i suoi
possibili rimedi.

Back in 1850 when California became the 31st
state of the Union, the historic memory of the
USA lost definitely the myth of the far west.
Two oceans as boundaries and huge fenceless
land. Maybe as destiny or as vocation in
California the american dream is pushed to go
"over", a step beyond the border of ordinary
life. An invisible rope ties our story to this
destiny. The place is San Francisco, flower
blossomed upon the ocean, here the ballad of
the "grateful dead" starts and takes rhyme, all
so deep in the past of our heart
that seems today.
While a big part of the USA is dreaming in the
dream of welfare, another is awake and leaves
for a new goldrush.
The "Renaissance" that blossoms in San
Francisco in the first part of the sixties is deeply
rooted in the beat circuit of the fifties. In this
neighborhood people like Kerouac,
Burroughs, Ginsberg, Corso and many other
children of the setting sun have found a home.
North Beach was the headquarter of the
Beatniks while the City
Light Bookstore, owned by
Lawrence Ferlinghetti, was the destination of
the new literature. As a bolt in a clear sky here
comes the visions of the great psychedelic
father, Aldous Huxley. It is 1954 when the old
literary and philosopher writes *Doors of
perceptions*, first parable of the mystic
chemistry. In this climate in the late 1959 at the
Veteran Hospital in Menlo Park begun a series
of research on the effects of LSD.
That was a governmental research program on
schizophrenia and on its cure.
In these experiments psycotrophic substances
were given to volunteers and the reaction was
then studied. Part of this scene were Ken
Kesey, author of *One flew over the cuckoo nest*,

Durante le varie sedute di sperimentazione venivano somministrate ai volontari una serie di sostanze psicotrope delle quali veniva poi studiata la reazione sul soggetto. Parte di questa scena furono lo scrittore Ken Kesey, autore di *Qualcuno Volò sul Nido del Cuculo*, e Robert Hunter, futuro paroliere dei Grateful Dead.
Un laboratorio medico è però troppo piccolo e asettico per esperimenti che scavano l'universo della coscienza, così Kesey ed altri alchimisti dello spirito decidono di continuare in proprio la ricerca. A La Honda, tra le montagne della contea di Santa Cruz e nel fitto dei boschi, nasce la comune Merry Pranksters. Ad essa presto si uniscono menti strane e bizzarre come quelle di August Owsley Stanley III, mago dell'LSD e del suono, e Neal Cassidy, santone beat consegnato alla storia come Dean Moriarty, personaggio attorno a cui ruota *On the Road* di Jack Kerouac.
Tra i frequentatori del ritiro di La Honda vi era anche una band appena votatasi al suono elettrico, i *Warlocks*, composta da *Jerry Garcia, Phil Lesh, Bob Weir, Ron "Pig Pen" Mc Kernan* e *Bill Kreutzmann* (alias Bill Sommers). A questo nucleo originario, i futuri Grateful Dead arrivarono dopo un esordio di stampo tradizionale nel circuito folk e bluegrass che animava le coffehouses di San Francisco. In particolare alla scuola bluegrass era cresciuto Jerry Garcia, suonatore di banjo che aveva militato in diverse formazioni nei primi anni '60. I nomi di quei giorni erano *Bob and Jerry, Thunder Mtn. Tub Thumpers, Hart Valley Drifters, Wildwood Boys, Zodiacs, Sleepy Hollow Hog Stompers, Black Mountain Boys, Mother Mc Trees Uptown Jug Champions*.
L'idea di formare una band elettrica fu di Pig Pen, che dal padre, noto DJ della Bay Area, aveva ereditato l'amore per il blues. Su questa strada muove i primi passi frequentando clubs come il *Boar's Head*, il *Tangent*, e lo *Chateau* dove appunto ha il primo incontro con Garcia.

Jerry Garcia, 1965

Phil Lesh, 1965

Pig Pen & Bob Weir, 1965

Bill Kreutzmann, 1965

and Robert Hunter, later wordsmith of the Grateful Dead.

A medical laboratory is too small and aseptic for experiment in the universe of human mind, so Kesey and other spirit 's alchemists decided to follow the research by themselves. At La Honda, deep in the mountains of the Santa Cruz county, hidden in the woods, the commune of the *Merry Pranksters* was born. Very soon other odd and strange minds, like *August Stanley Owsey III*, sound and LSD magician, and Neal Cassady, beat high priest well known to the history as Dean Moriarty of Jack Kerouac's *On the road* fame, gather to the Pranksters.

Among the people who were in La Honda there was a band just turned electric, the Warlocks. *The Warlocks* were *Jerry Garcia, Phil Lesh, Bob Weir, Ron "Pig Pen" McKernan* and *Bill Kreutzmann*. At this stage, the future Grateful Dead, arrives after a long time of playing in Folk and Bluegrass clubs and coffehouses in San Francisco.

In the Bluegrass school Jerry Garcia was grown as a banjo player that have been part of several combos in the early '60.

The names were *Bob and Jerry, Thunder Mountain Tub Thumpers, Hart Valley Drifters, Wildwood Boys, Zodiacs, Sleepy Hollow Hog Stompers, Black Mountain Boys, Mother McCree's Uptown Jug Champions*.

Pig Pen got the idea of forming an electric band. Pig had inherited the love for the blues from his father, well known DJ in the Bay Area.

On this road he starts to walk in the clubs like *Boar's Head, Tangent* and the *Chateau* where he meets Jerry Garcia. It is late autumn of 1964 when the Pig Pen's project is complete.

The times goes that way and from everywhere comes positive signals, as the release of the first major movie by the Beatles *A hard days night*. So the original Jug Band gets electric and lands to the Ken Kesey court, becoming the "houseband".

E' il tardo autunno del 1964 quando il progetto di Pig Pen si realizza. I tempi parlavano in quel senso e da molte parti venivano segnali di conferma, come l'uscita del film *A hard day's night* dei Beatles. Così l'originaria Jug Band si elettrifica ed approda alla corte di Ken Kesey diventandone la *houseband*. Siamo nel 1965, gli esperimenti psichedelici si trasferiscono dalle campagne di La Honda ai centri urbani della West Coast. Nascono gli Acid Test, sorta di baccanale a base di LSD, Light Show, suoni, voci e ovviamente musica dei Grateful Dead. I Warlocks avevano cambiato il loro nome nel novembre del 1965 poiché già un'altra band si chiamava in quel modo. Il nome fu trovato per caso aprendo un dizionario a casa di Phil Lesh, quella scritta a lettere d'oro sul *Funk & Wagnall's Dictionary* fu per Garcia e soci un fulmine di energia positiva conservata poi negli anni. Col nuovo nome i Grateful Dead passano la fondamentale esperienza degli Acid Test. Ufficialmente l'era dei sensi ribelli si apre il 4 dicembre 1965 a San Josè, il primo Acid Test nasce subito dopo il concerto tenuto dai Rolling Stones quella sera. L'ultimo fu il 2 ottobre 1966 alla San Francisco State University Cafeteria; quattro giorni dopo, il 6 ottobre 1966, l'LSD divenne illegale in California. E' in questo arco di tempo che avviene la svolta fondamentale: l'originaria Jug Band si trasforma e nascono le atmosfere sperimentali e dilatate che ancora oggi contrassegnano i Grateful Dead.

We're in 1965, the psychedelic experiments are transferred from the wood of La Honda to the urban neigborhood of the west coast. The *Acid Test* was born.
The Acid test was some sort of LSD orgy, light shows, sounds, voices and, obviously, the music of Grateful Dead.
The Warlocks had to change their name in November 1965 because there was yet another band with that name.
The name was found by chance opening a dictionary at Phil Lesh's home.
Those word on the "Funk & Wagnalls Standard Dictionary" seems burning gold to Garcia and friends and became a bolt of positive energy throughtout the years.
With the new name the *Grateful Dead* pass through the basic experience of the Acid Test. The age of rebellious senses is officially born on December 4, 1965 in San José, the first Acid Test was made just after the concert of the Rolling Stones that night.
The last was made on the night of December 2, 1966 at the San Francisco State University Cafeteria.
Four days later, on October 6, 1966, the LSD became illegal in the state of California. Within this time there is the turning point, the originary Jug band is transformed and the enlarged experimental atmospheres that still today are part of the Grateful Dead were born.

KLOSTERMANS 89

THE GOLDEN ROAD: TO UNLIMITED DEVOTION

L'America post-colombiana ha due figure originali nella storia del suo costume: il cow-boy e l'Hippy. Fu l'introduzione del filo spinato a cancellare il primo creando recinti sicuri come fortezze, del secondo é restato lo spirito pacifico e luminoso, forse in pochi, sicuramente in molti Deadheads.

Haight-Hashbury non é solo il nome di due strade ma é di più il nome della festa hippy che anima San Francisco tra il '65 e il '67. I Grateful Dead sono parte del mosaico psichedelico e del nuovo umanesimo che in quegli anni prende vita. Un respiro nuovo attraversa la coscienza dell'America e trova dimora a San Francisco. Nuove e pacifiche comunità fioriscono spontaneamente, dando vita ad innumerevoli esperienze. I *Diggers*, in omaggio ai loro omonimi del secolo prima, sono una comune filantropica e di assistenza; l'*Oracle* e il *Berkeley Barb* sono mirabili esempi di stampa underground; la *Family Dog* perla e genio nella gestione della nuova scena musicale; lo *Psychedelic Shop* dei fratelli Thielin e via dicendo sono solo alcuni esempi dei fermenti di quell'epoca.

Uno dei momenti più alti di questa esperienza é toccato sabato 14 gennaio 1967. I Jefferson Airplane immortaleranno l'evento in una delle loro canzoni più belle: *Won't you try - Saturday Afternoon*. In una chiara giornata di sole invernale si tiene lo "Human Be-In: a gathering of tribes". E' l'incontro delle nuove tribù psichedeliche, *"il gioioso faccia a faccia che dà inizio ad una nuova epoca"*, come recita un volantino di quei giorni. Ai Polo Fields, nel cuore del Golden Gate Park, qualcuno prova così a lavare la vita e il destino, ed a danzare in cerchio si ritrovano in tanti: *Timothy Leary, Allen Ginsberg, Gary Snider, Jerry Rubin* ed un pò tutti i teatranti della nuova generazione.

Post columbian america has only two original figures in his costume: the Cow-boy and the Hippy. As the introduction of barbed wire, creating fences safe as fortress, put apart the first, the second left us a light and peaceful spirit, maybe in few, but surely in many Deadheads.

Haight-Asbury is not only the name of two streets but mostly it is the name of the hippy party that gave life to San Francisco between '65 and '67. The Grateful Dead are part of the psychedelic mosaic and the new reinnassance that took form in those years. A new breath comes across America's conscience and finds a home in San Francisco. New and peaceful communes bloom giving life to numberless experiences. *The Diggers*, in homage to their epigones of a century ago, are a philantropic helping commune; the *Oracle* and the *Berkeley Barb* are extraordinary examples of underground press; the *Family Dog*, gem and genius in organizing the new musical scene; brothers Thielin's own *Psychedelic Shop* and so on are only few examples of theturmoil of that time. One of the highest points of these experiences is the day of January 14, 1967. The *Jefferson Airplane* immortalizes this event in one of their finest songs *Won't you try/ Saturday afternoon*.

In a clear sunny day the Human Be-In is held; a gathering of the tribes, is the meeting of the psychedelic tribes, *"the joyous face to face who start a new age"*, as been printed a flyer of that days. At the Polo Fields, in the heart of the Golden Gate Park, someone tries to wash clean life and destiny.

Dancing around you could find a lot of people: *Timothy Leary, Allen Ginsberg, Gary Snyder, Jerry Rubin* and all of the main attraction of the new generation.

Tra costumi, campanelli, cimbali, tamburi e fiori anche le maggiori bands di Frisco (*Grateful Dead, Jefferson Airplane, Quicksilver Messenger Service, Big Brother & the Holding Co.*) si uniscono alla festa.

Sotto questo cielo di belle speranze si apre l'anno in cui tutti berranno il vino delle fate. Il 1° giugno esce il nuovo e atteso album dei Beatles, *Sgt. Pepper's Lonely Hearts Club Band*. E' il segnale inequivocabile di un cambiamento nella musica, nel costume e nel pensiero.

Il battesimo psichedelico del gruppo che ha segnato la nascita della musica popolare moderna é una fondamentale conferma per il popolo di California.

Dal 16 al 18 giugno 1967 si tiene a Monterey, California, il primo Festival in assoluto della storia del Rock. Il marchio di quei giorni scriverà col fuoco tre nomi nel libro d'oro della musica: *Jimi Hendrix, Janis Joplin e Otis Redding*. I Grateful Dead suonano il giorno 18 e del loro set resta qualche traccia solo su bootleg come la furiosa versione di *Viola Lee Blues*.

All'epoca il fenomeno californiano è ancora una cosa locale, ma lo sarà per poco. Il 5 luglio 1967 il Time Magazine dedica la sua copertina agli Hippies: *The Hippies: Anatomy of a Sub-Culture*. Da ogni parte del paese comincia l'esodo verso San Francisco: qui si riversa ogni tipo di avanguardia cui si aggiungono, purtroppo, cialtroni e trafficanti di ogni genere. I media si sono ormai impadroniti della nascente controcultura. La storiografia ufficiale qui parla della *Summer of Love*, in realtà l'estate dell'amore é a questo punto definitivamente morta. Il 6 ottobre 1967 i Diggers ed altre centinaia di persone celebrano la *Morte dell'Hippy*, una parata ed una cerimonia che si chiudono con il funerale fatto all'insegna dello Psychedelic Shop. Un simbolismo, come i tanti dell'epoca, per indicare la fine ideale di un periodo retto dalla transitoria giovinezza della speranza.

Among costumes, bells, cymbals, drums and flowers all the major San Franciscan rock bands, *Grateful Dead, Jefferson Airplane, Quicksilver Messenger Service, Big Brother & the Holding Company* gather for the feast.

Under this sky, lightened by rays of hopes, when everyone will drink the magic wine of the fairy tales, the new year began. On June 1 the new and long awaited Beatles album *Sgt. Pepper's lonely hearts club band* is released.

It is the start of a change in popular music, in the way of living and thinking. The psychedelic baptism from the group that has marked the birth of the modern popular music is an affirmation for the California people.

From June 16 to June 18, 1967 in Monterey, California, the absolute first Festival in rock history was held. The mark of those days will write with fire the names in music's own golden book, *Jimi Hendrix, Janis Joplin* and *Otis Redding*. The Grateful Dead played on the 18 and from their set remains only few tracks on bootlegs album, like the wild edition of *Viola Lee blues*.

At that time the california wonder is only a local new but it will remain unknown for a short time.

On July 5, 1967, Time magazine devotes its cover to the Hippies, *The Hippies: Anatomy of a Sub-culture*. From every part of the country began the exodus to San Francisco. There pours every kind of avant garde adding, unfortunately, charlatans and traffikers. Mass comunication began the owners of the new counter-culture. The official history put in this place starts off the *Summer of Love*, really at this point the summer has already turned to winter. On october 6, 1967 the Diggers and other hundreds of people celebrates the *Death of the Hippy*, a symbolic parade that ends with the funeral of the Psychedelic Shops sign. A symbol, like others of the times, to show the end of a period ruled by the temporary youth of hope.

Tra l'attivismo dei radicali, intenti a cambiare il mondo, e la contemplazione degli Hippies, intenti a cambiare le loro teste, la musica va avanti e segna una sua linea originale. In questo senso la Family Dog ha senza dubbio un merito innegabile, quello di aver aperto una stagione nuova di zecca nella gestione ed organizzazione delle attività concertistiche. La comune, nata da un'idea di *Luria Castell, Ellen Hammond* ed *Al Kelly*, apre la stagione delle *Dance-Hall*. E' un pomeriggio di ottobre quando i tre si recano in visita da Ralph J. Gleason per esporre il loro progetto. Scriverà poi Gleason: *"I tempi erano maturi per danzare, non per le strade come nella canzone di Martha and the Vandellas, ma da qualche parte"*. Ed in effetti ciò fu vero. Le parole di Luria Castell in quel pomeriggio di sole autunnale risultarono profetiche: *"San Francisco può essere la Liverpool americana"*. *"Ci sono abbastanza talenti qui, specialmente nel campo della folk music. Noi non abbiamo particolari gruppi da presentare, ma solo un progetto che sta per partire, conoscere, informarci e divertirci col Rock'n'Roll"*.

In a place between the radical activisms of the politicos, while they were trying to change the world, and the pacific contemplation of the hippies, while changing their heads, the music goes straight ahead and follows an original line. In this way the Family Dog doubtless has a merit opening a brand new age in organizing the dance concerts. This commune, born from an idea of *Luria Castell, Ellen Hammond* and *Alton Kelley* opens the season of the *Dance-Hall*. In a afternoon in October they go to the office of Ralph J. Gleason to show him their project. Later Gleason will write: *"The time were right for dancing, not in the street as in theMartha and the Vandellas'song, but somewhere"*. Few thing has been said truer than this. The words spoken by Luria Castell that afternoon sound like a prophecy: *"San Francisco could be the American Liverpool"*. *"There's enough talent here, especially in the folk-music field. We don't have any particular group to present, just a plan to get started, to acquire knowledge, information and have fun with a rock'n'roll sound"*.

Grateful Dead, 1967

"Il Rock'n'Roll é la nuova forma di comunicazione per la nostra generazione".
"La musica é la più bella via di comunicazione, é la via sulla quale ci avviamo a cambiare le cose".
Così la Family Dog tiene il suo primo Dance Concert alla Longshoreman's Hall il 16 ottobre 1965. Il poster di quel giorno recita: "A Rock'n'Roll Dance and Concert".
Aprirono così le danze Jefferson Airplane, The Marbles e i Great Society.
Nasce in questo contesto il San Francisco Sound e le varie sale da ballo che ne segnerano le tappe e l'avventura: il *Fillmore Auditorium*, l'*Avalon Ballroom*, il *Carousell Ballroom*, autogestito per un breve periodo da Grateful Dead e Jefferson Airplane e poi rilevato da *Bill Graham* che ne farà il mitico *Fillmore West*.
Per finire il *Winterland*, ultimo e più longevo dei locali di San Francisco che chiuderà i battenti per il New Year's Eve '78 con un'indimenticabile performance dei Grateful Dead.
Opera fondamentale di questo periodo é *The Jefferson Airplane and the San Francisco Sound*, libro del già citato Ralph J. Gleason.
E' proprio costui, futuro fondatore di *Rolling Stone* ed all'epoca critico jazz di Down Beat e del San Francisco Chronicle, ad intuire e capire la novità che stava nascendo a San Francisco.
Centinaia di bands animavano le notti della baia, dalle tradizionali basi del folk e del blues nascono sonorità zeppe di nuove emozioni, colme di profumi e colori vividi.
E' un viaggio onirico a ritroso che tocca gli archetipi della coscienza.
Su questo grande mare della nuova musica veglia la sacra trimurti del San Francisco sound:
Grateful Dead,
Jefferson Airplane,
Quicksilver Messenger Service.

"Rock'n'roll is the new form of communication for our generation".
"Music is the most beautiful way to communicate, it's the way we're going to change things".
So the Family Dog held its first "Dance-Concert" at the Longshoreman's Hall on October 16, 1965. The poster of the event says: "A rock'n'roll Dance and Concert", the dance was opened by *Jefferson Airplane*, the *Marbles* and the *Great Society*.
This contest gave life to the San Francisco's Sound and the various dance halls that there were in the town: the *Fillmore Auditorium*, the *Avalon Ballroom*, the *Carousell Ballroom*, for a brief moment owned by Grateful Dead and Jefferson Airplane then owned by Bill Graham that will transform it in the mythic *Fillmore West*. At last the *Winterland*, the most long-lived San Francisco hall, that will close down on the 1978 New Years eve with an unforgettable performance of the Grateful Dead.
The best book on this moment is *The Jefferson Airplane and San Francisco Sound*, a book by the yet named *Ralph J. Gleason*.
It was Ralph J. Gleason itself, future founder of *Rolling Stone Magazine* and at the time jazz reviewer of *Down Beat* and the *San Francisco Chronicle*, to perceive the news that were rising from San Francisco.
Hundreds of bands were playing in the clubs at night in the bay area, from the basis of the folk and blues music emerges new sound full of new emotions filled of perfumes and vivid colors.
It's a dream trip to the back that touches the ground of conscience.
On this ocean of new music the sacred trinurti of the sound of San Francisco arises:
Grateful Dead,
Jefferson Airplane,
Quicksilver Messenger Service.

710 ASHBURY STREET

Ai primi del 1966 i Dead tentano la carta musicale di Los Angeles ma, insoddisfatti, nel giugno dello stesso anno rientrano a San Francisco. Trascorrono l'estate a Marin County e nei primi giorni di settembre si trasferiscono in una vecchia palazzina di stile vittoriano al 710 di Ashbury Street. Qui vivranno in comunità fino al marzo 1968. In breve tempo il posto diventa ritrovo abituale di altri gruppi: Jefferson Airplane, Big Brother & the Holding Co., Quicksilver Messenger Service, Charlatans. Artisti come *Stanley Mouse*, pranksters di antica memoria come *Carolyn Adams*, conosciuta come *Mountain Girl*, compagna di Garcia, Owsley ed una tribù di gente colorata affollano le scale di questo antico edificio.

Intanto, su un altro fronte, le grandi compagnie discografiche fiutano l'affare che viene dalla Bay Area. Il primo gruppo ad avere un contratto sono i Jefferson Airplane che firmano per la RCA, seguono poi Grateful Dead, Big Brother, Quicksilver e così via.

Nel marzo 1967 esce per la Warner Bros. l'album di esordio del gruppo: *The Grateful Dead* viene registrato in soli tre giorni agli RCA studios di Los Angeles. Il risultato é decisamente inferiore a quello che il gruppo avrebbe potuto esprimere, colpa della fretta e della poca familiarità col lavoro in studio. Il materiale registrato comprende canzoni del repertorio usualmente eseguito tra la fine del '66 e gli inizi del '67. Il suono é asciutto e cadenzato e senza elementi di novità, unica eccezione *Viola Lee Blues*, impregnata di psichedelia e vera gemma del disco. Tra le due composizioni del gruppo *The Golden Road* è senz'altro quella più fresca e colorata; nelle sue parole si legge tutta l'atmosfera e la spensieratezza dei giorni dell'Haight Ashbury. Il 29 settembre 1967 alla line-up del gruppo si aggiunge un sesto uomo, *Mickey Hart*,

In the early days of 1966 the Grateful Dead were trying a deal in Los Angeles, unsatisfied, in June they head back to San Francisco. The summer sees them in Marin County and in September they all moved in an old victorian house at 710 Ashbury Street. There they lived until March 1968. Just few days afterthe place is transformed in the meeting point of other musical groups, *Jefferson Airplane, Big Brother & the Holding Company, Quicksilver Messenger Service, Charlatans.* Painters as *Stanley Mouse*, old time prankster like *Caroline Adams*, a.k.a. *Mountain Girl* the Jerry Garcia fiancée, Owsley and a wonderful, colorful tribe gathers on the stairs of this ancient house.

Meanwhile, in another side, the major record companies smelled money coming from the Bay Area. The very first group that signs a contract is the Jefferson Airplane for RCA, then comes the Grateful Dead, Big Brother & the Holding Company, Quicksilver and so on.

In March 1967 the first album of the group: *The Grateful Dead*, recorded in three days only at the RCA studios in Los Angeles, is released by Warner Brothers Records. The results is a lower degree of what the group could play, due to the hurry and the unknown of the recording studio.

The tracks recorded are songs performed usually between the end of '66 and the early '67. The sound is rhythmical dry without new things, the only one exception is *Viola Lee blues*, a blues song imbued with psychedelia.

Among the group's own composition *The Golden Road* is doubtlessly the fresher and the most colorful one, in its words you can find all the atmosphere and the gayness of the Haigh-Asbury days. On September 29, 1967 the group line-up is increased by a sixth man, *Mickey Hart*, Bill Kreutzman's teacher. The coming of a new drummer implies a major

già istruttore di Bill Kreutzmann. L'arrivo di una nuova batteria determina un'ulteriore caratterizzazione del suono e del ritmo.
"Non cercavamo di essere due batteristi, ma uno solo con otto braccia", così Kreutzmann ricorda quel momento.
Arriva intanto un'altra pedina fondamentale, il poeta e liricista Robert Hunter, amico di vecchia data di Garcia che si unisce alla band e ne diventa il paroliere. Uno dei primi frutti del nuovo connubio é *Dark Star*, brano in cui si miscelano alla perfezione la visionarietà delle parole e quella della musica.
Anthem of the Sun, secondo album, esce nel giugno del 1968. E' ancora una prova deludente che non rende giustizia a quanto i Dead riescono ad esprimere dal vivo.
Proprio per ricreare l'atmosfera live il gruppo decide di adottare una particolare tecnica di registrazione.
Gli shows tra il novembre del 1967 e l'aprile del 1968 vengono registrati in due modi diversi: in diretta dal mixer su un otto piste e, contemporaneamente, da un quattro piste che cattura invece il suono della sala.
Le due versioni mixate insieme sono poi il risultato finale.
The Other One é il frutto di questo esperimento, interessante tecnicamente ma dai risultati decisamente lontani dal suono viscerale che i Dead esprimono in concerto.
Il brano in questione é allo stesso tempo un affresco che ricorda la saga degli Acid Test ed é anche una dedica a Neal Cassady, morto agli inizi del 1968 in circostanze misteriose. Alla realizzazione delle parti in studio di *Anthem of the Sun* partecipa un settimo elemento che dalla fine del '68 si unirà per un breve periodo ai Dead. *Tom Costanten*, ex compagno di stanza di Phil Lesh, é un pianista dal viaggio sperimentale, particolarmente attento alle avanguardie elettroniche. Suo é appunto il "prepared piano" presente nel disco.

characterization of the rhythm and in the sound. *"We didn't try to be two different drummers, but only one with eight arms"*, in this way Kreutzmann remembers that day.
In those days another piece is added to the group, the poet and lyricist *Robert Hunter*, old friend of Garcia that joins the band and becomes the wordsmith. One of the first piece wrote for the band is *Dark Star*, a track of perfect blend of words and visionarity in music.
Anthem of the sun, second album, is released in June 1968. It is another delusion that simply it is not fair to the live Grateful Dead. Trying to recreate the "live" atmosphere the group tried a new way of recording. The shows recorded between November 1967 and April 1968 are taped in two different ways: straight from a soundboard and from another source recording the reflection of the sound in the room. The two recordings, mixed together are the final result. *The Other One* is the fruit of this experiment, interesting in a technical way, but the results, once again, are very far from the visceral sound that the Dead had in live concerts. This track is a paint that remembers the sage of the "acid tests" and is dedicated to Neal Cassady too (Cassady died in mysterious circumstances that year). At the studio recording of *Anthem of the Sun* a new man participates, *Tom Constanten*, that will join the band for a brief time at the end of '68. Constanten was an old Phil Lesh's room-mate, and is a sperimental musician, particularly in the field of electronic music. It's him who plays the "prepared piano" on the record.
Aoxomoxoa comes in June 1969 and is another step toward new experimental techniques. It differs from the previous album, this one has no "live contaminations", it is a brand new studio album recorded for the first time on an eight tracks machine. The scarce approach to the electronics and the mixture of different styles make this album another failure.

710 Ashbury Street, 1966

Aoxomoxoa é del giugno 1969 e rappresenta un nuovo passo verso tecniche sperimentali. A differenza del precedente album che viveva di contaminazioni live, il nuovo é rigorosamente frutto del lavoro in studio. L'approccio scarso con l'elettronica e la miscela di stili differenti segnano un altro passo falso. *St. Stephen* e *China Cat Sunflower* sono le canzoni più accessibili che poi diverranno classiche live-songs della band. L'arrivo di Costanten e la completa assenza delle parti vocali fanno di questo album un disco orfano di Pig Pen.

Il 16 agosto 1969 i Grateful Dead sono a Woodstock, ma é un giorno da dimenticare. Il concerto si tiene nel bel mezzo di un temporale notturno con il gruppo completamente terrorizzato dalle violente scariche elettriche che avvolgono il palco traballante. Bob Weir cadrà a terra semisvenuto. E' davvero un brutto concerto, e così il gruppo decide di non apparire tanto nel disco quanto nel film.

St. Stephen and *China cat sunflower* are the most accessible songs that become later stapples in the band live repertoire. The arrival of Constanten and the completely lacks of his vocals made this an album orphan of Pig Pen. On August 16, 1969, the Grateful Dead are in Woodstock Festival, but it's a bad day. They will play in the midst of a storm weather with the group scared to death from the terrible bolt that tangles the collapsing stage. Bob Weir will faint after being struck by electricity. It is a bad performance so they decide not to appear in the record and in the movie from that festival. In the mean time the economic position of the group became really bad. After the scarce sale of the records the Warner Bros. pushed the boys in releasing a live recording. In this way *Live/Dead* is born as a light epitaph of the psychedelic sage.

Intanto la situazione economica si era seriamente compromessa a causa delle deludenti prove discografiche ed é la stessa Warner Bros. a fare pressioni per un disco live. Nasce in questo clima il *Live Dead*, epitaffio luminoso dell'epoca psichedelica. Il doppio disco riporta estratti dagli spettacoli tenuti al Fillmore West tra il 27 febbraio ed il 2 marzo 1969. Impressionante ed inevitabile é il paragone con i dischi in studio. Pur essendo l'album fuori da ogni logica commerciale, *Live Dead* rende giustizia alla magia espressiva che nasce in concerto. Le canzoni sono riportate sul vinile senza alcun editing e fotografano appieno i terreni più congeniali al gruppo. I 21 minuti di *Dark Star* parlano da soli, spazi sterminati su cui la chitarra di Garcia disegna arabeschi di rara bellezza. Tutto il ritmo, la potenza ed il valore della band eruttano dai solchi del disco, indimenticabile *Turn On Your Lovelight* nella versione più bella che Pig Pen ci ha lasciato. *Live Dead* é il testamento spirituale ed il marchio proprio che i Grateful Dead lasciano degli anni '60. I tempi erano in movimento, al vento caldo delle notti psichedeliche si sovrapponeva la brezza fresca e leggera figlia di sogni più genuini ed intimisti.

This double record album contains the extracts of shows held at the Fillmore West and at the Avalon Ballroom between February 27 and March 2, 1969.
Impressive is the comparison with the studio albums.
Although out of any commercial logic, *Live/Dead* finally shows the magic of a live concert by the band.
The songs had been transferred to vinyl without editing at all, and made clear pictures of the places where the band is in live performance.
The 23 minutes of live re-edition of *Dark Star* talks by themselves, limitless spaces where the Garcia's guitar paint arabesques of rare beauty.
All the rhythm, the power and the bravery of the band comes out from the record's grooves.
It is unforgettable the best *Turn on your lovelight* that Pig Pen has left to us.
Live/dead is the spiritual testament and the mark that the Grateful Dead leaves in the sixties.
The times were changing and at the warm winds of the psychedelic nights a light, cool breeze, made of genuine and more intimate dreams begun to superimpose.

Grateful Dead with Tom Costanten at the time of "Live/Dead"

PASS HERE AND GO ON, YOU ARE ON THE ROAD FOR THE PARADISE NOW

In aprile Garcia aveva comprato una pedal steel guitar, passando poi molte notti dell'estate '69 insieme ad un amico degli esordi, *John "Marmaduke" Dawson*. Col leader dei *New Riders of the Purple Sage* spazia nel vecchio repertorio folk, country e bluegrass.

Intanto il quartier generale dei Dead non é più al 710 di Ashbury Street ma al *The Barn*, il ranch di Mickey Hart a Novato, in piena campagna. Frequentatori della residenza campestre erano all'epoca anche *David Crosby, Stephen Stills e Graham Nash*. Proprio con questi ultimi la band comincia a lavorare seriamente sulle parti vocali e i risultati di quei giorni sono immortalati nelle gemme elettro-acustiche dei due album successivi.

Workingman's Dead esce nel maggio del 1970 e *American Beauty* nel novembre dello stesso anno: é il tempo del ritorno alle radici e coincide col momento più creativo in assoluto della band. Passate le ombre calde e la giovinezza psichedelica, i Grateful Dead si avventurano lungo i sentieri della paglia e del fieno. Figli della splendida intesa tra la melodia luminosa di Garcia e la grande vena poetica di Hunter, nascono in questo momento rose e canzoni intramontabili: *Uncle John's Band, Casey Jones, Box of Rain, Sugar Magnolia, Truckin', Ripple*. Il suono si fa nitido e chiaro come un cielo sereno, i Dead traducono nella propria lingua le parole che furono del più nobile passato della musica americana.

L'anno in corso é segnato anche dal successo del tour *An Evening with the Grateful Dead and New Riders of the Purple Sage*. Lo show é diviso in tre parti: nella prima sono i NRPS ad esibirsi con il loro classico country-rock arricchito dal fine lavoro di Garcia alla pedal steel.

In April 1969 Garcia had bought a "pedal steel guitar" passing several nights of the summer of '69 together with an old time friend of his, *John "Marmaduke" Dawson*. With the leader of the *New Riders of the Purple Sage* he plays the old repertoire of folk, country and bluegrass music. The headquarter of the Dead is no more at 710 Ashbury Street, but it has smoved to *The Barn*, the Mickey Hart ranch in Novato, out in the country. Habituees of this residence were *David Crosby, Stephen Stills* and *Graham Nash*. With them the band starts to work seriously on the vocal parts of the songs, and the results are immortalized on the electro-acoustic gems of the two following albums.

Workingman's dead is released on May 1970 and *American Beauty* on November of the same year. It's the time to get back to the roots and it coincides with the best moment of the band as a composing unit.

After warm shadows and the psychedelic youth the Grateful Dead dare on the paths of hay and straw. Sons of the splendid togetherness of Garcia light melody and great poetic heart of Hunter, this moment gave life to roses and indelible songs: *Uncle John's band, Casey Jones, Box of rain, Sugar Magnolia, Truckin', Ripple*. The sound is clear and tidy as the sky, the Dead translate in their own language the words coming from the noblesse of americana.

This year is marked from the huge success of the tour *An evening with the Grateful Dead and New Riders of the Purple Sage* too. The show is divided in three different parts. In the first part the *NRPS* perform their classic country-rock, embelled by the fine work of Garcia on pedal steel guitar.

Seguono un set acustico ed uno elettrico dei Dead. Nel febbraio 1970 Mickey Hart lascia il gruppo, ufficialmente per seguire le proprie ricerche musicali che culmineranno poi in *Rolling Thunder*, suo primo lavoro solista datato 1972. In realtà l'abbandono é legato anche alla fuga del padre, Lenny Hart, con buona parte dei guadagni dei Dead.

A Lenny Hart, all'epoca cassiere del gruppo, verrà poi ironicamente dedicata la canzone *He's Gone*.

Skullfuck doveva essere il titolo dell'album che esce nell'autunno del 1971, ma l'opposizione della Warner Bros. fa sì che il nome sia semplicemente *Grateful Dead*.

Il doppio live, ribattezzato *Skull and Roses* per la copertina che richiama uno dei loro poster più famosi, conferma la trascinante potenza live del gruppo. Garcia commenterà: *"Siamo noi! E' il prototipo dei Grateful Dead. La lezione base"*.

Then follows an acoustic and an electric set by the Dead.

In February 1971 Mickey Hart leaves the group, officially for pursuing his musical research that will lead to *Rolling Thunder*, his first solo album of 1972. The other cause for leaving is the fact that the father of Mickey, Lenny, at the time manager of the group, left with a good slice of the group money. The song *He's gone* will be ironically dedicated to Lenny Hart.

The title for the next album, released in autumn 1971, should have to be *Skullfuck*, but the opposition of Warner Bros. is strong, so the group rename it simply *Grateful Dead*.

The double live record, nicknamed *Skull and Roses* from the cover that is one of the most famous poster of the Dead, is a confirmation of their live power. Garcia will say about it: *"It's us, man. It's the prototype Grateful Dead. Basic unit"*.

The Skullfuck band

Accanto a standards come *Not Fade Away/ Going down the Road Feelin' Bad* e *Me and Bobby McGee* vengono introdotte nuove e stupende canzoni come *Bertha, Playing in the band* e la struggente ballata *Wharf Rat. Skull and Roses* é il primo disco d'oro dei Grateful Dead. Il cielo intanto si ammanta di nuvole tetre, un'ala gelida e nera vola sull'aura del morto riconoscente. Pig Pen si ammala seriamente a causa degli eccessi alcolici e salta diversi concerti costringendo i Dead a chiamare come rinforzo il pianista *Keith Godchaux* (chiusa la parentesi con Tom Costanten, separatosi amichevolmente nel gennaio '70, erano restati senza un ottimo pianista e tastierista). Le virtù di Pig Pen erano altre e stavano nella potente presenza scenica, nel ruggito poderoso della voce e nel gran feeling che ne animava le interpretazioni. Pur malato, si riunisce in dicembre alla band, cui si era aggiunta come vocalist *Donna Godchaux*, moglie di Keith. Il 1972 é per i Grateful Dead l'anno delle stelle comete. A gennaio esce il primo disco solo di Garcia; l'omonimo lavoro del "maestro", successivamente ribattezzato *The Wheel*, é un capolavoro immune alla corrosione ed al fluire del tempo. Uscisse oggi, dopo vent'anni, avrebbe lo stesso profumo di petali alati, tali sono le sue canzoni che in breve diventeranno classici dei Dead: *Deal, Bird Song, Sugaree, Loser, The Wheel*. Jerry fa tutto da solo, suona tutti gli strumenti con il solo aiuto di Bill Kreutzmann alla batteria. Nello stesso anno un'altra foglia d'oro si posa in terra, dopo l'esordio di Garcia é Weir a venire allo scoperto col suo primo solo. *Ace* può essere però considerato a tutti gli effetti un disco dei Grateful Dead, stante la partecipazione della band al completo. Anche qui il colpo é centrato: *Greatest Story Ever Told, Black Throated Wind, One More Saturday Night, Cassidy* e su tutte *Looks like rain* sono altrettante perle che si aggiungono al repertorio dei Dead.

Side by side to standards like *Not fade away/ Going down the road feeling bad* and *Me & Bobby McGee* we could find new and fantastic songs like *Bertha, Playing in the band* and the struggling ballad *Wharf rat. Skull and Roses* is the first Grateful Dead golden album. The sky is being filled by black clouds, an ice cold wing flies on the grateful dead aura. Pig Pen gets seriously ill and, due to alcoholic excesses, does not play in some concerts. The Dead chose as substitute *Keith Godchaux* (Tom Constanten left the group in a friendly way in January 1970) because they needed a good piano and keyboard player. The virtues of Pig Pen were others as the exuberant scenic presence, the powerful roar of his voice and the enormous feeling of his performances. Although he is ill, he joins the band again in December, together with the wife of Keith, *Donna Jean*, as vocalists. 1972 is for the Grateful Dead the year of the comet stars. In January the first Garcia album simply under the name of the "maestro", then called *The wheel* is released. It is a truly masterpiece immune to the time corrosion in the years. If it will be released today, after twenty years, it should have the same smell of winged petals, as its songs that will become stapples in the Dead concerts: *Deal, Bird song, Sugaree, Loser, The wheel*. Jerry does everything on his own, plays every instrument with the only help of Bill Kreutzman at the drums. In the same year another golden leaf land on the ground. After the début of Garcia it is Bob Weir that comes with his first solo album. But *Ace* could be considered a Grateful Dead album, as all the band, except Pig Pen, plays in the record. Here too the shot is in the core: *Greatest story ever told, Black throated wind, one more saturday night, Cassidy* and, over all, *Looks like rain*, with Garcia on the pedal steel guitar, are pearls that are added to the live repertoire of the band.

Ma l'avvenimento centrale dell'anno é sicuramente il tour europeo della primavera '72: per quasi due mesi i Dead scorazzano per il vecchio continente. Animati dallo spirito che fu già dei Pranksters, viaggiano con una carovana di oltre quaranta anime in due bus bizzarramente chiamati *Bozo* e *Bolo*. Il disco triplo, ancora una volta dal vivo, è chiamato *Europe '72* (questa volta il nome proposto dai Dead era "Europe on a 5,000 dollars a day" ma come al solito venne rifiutato dalla Warner Bros.) ed é il resoconto di questa avventura e la degna testimonianza dello stato di grazia del gruppo. Come non mai gli impasti vocali risultano armoniosi e perfettamente cuciti alla musica. *Europe '72* é un grande disco impreziosito da alcuni inediti decisamente belli ed efficaci: *Ramble On Rose, Tennessee Jed, Brown-Eyed Woman, Jack Straw, He's Gone.*

E' il 28 agosto 1972 a Veneta, nei boschi dell'Oregon. I Dead alzano la voce e chiamano per nome i ricordi solari degli anni '60. E' sicuramente uno dei concerti più belli mai tenuti dal gruppo, in un'atmosfera che ha le parole della magia e del sogno, il sole e la musica si fondono e con essi la danza di centinaia di Deadheads. *Sunshine Daydream* é un video che racconta di quel giorno lontano, doveva essere pubblicato ufficialmente ma il progetto non venne mai portato a termine. Il filmato é di una bellezza e suggestione rare e preziose, in particolare i quasi trenta minuti di *Dark Star* accompagnata dalla danza nuda dei presenti riportano il sogno ai giorni mai dimenticati di Haight-Ashbury.

But the main event of the year is surely the european tour of the spring 1972. For almost two months the Dead will travel on the old continent. Lively in the spirit of the Merry Pranksters they travel on two buses, the Bolo bus and the Bozo bus. The triple record set is once again recorded live and it is called *Europe '72* (the name this time proposed by the Dead was "Europe on a 5.000 dollars a day", but as usual the Warner Bros. rejected it) and is the perfect relation of this adventure and the deserving witness of the status in grace of the band. Never before the vocals had been so armonizing and perfectly tight to the music in live rendition. *Europe '72* is a great album made precious by some never before released songs that are truly live gems: *Ramble on Rose, Tennessee Jed, Brown eyed woman, Jack Straw, He's gone.*

On August 28, 1972, in Veneta, lost in the Oregon's woods, the Dead turn on the volume and recall by name the sunny remembrance of the sixties. It is surely one of the best concert ever made by them, in an atmosphere that has the words of magic, of the sun and the music blend together and with them the dance of hundreds of Deadheads.

Sunshine daydream is a movie that tells the story of that day, it should be officially released but the project had been shelved. The footage has a beauty and a charm that are both precious and rare, particularly the almost thirty minutes of *Dark Star*, while the naked audience dance keep the mind thinking of the never forgotten days of Haight-Asbury.

COME WITH ME OR GO ALONE

La scarsa familiarità con vincoli artistici e discografici, unita ad una naturale predisposizione all'autogestione, convincono la band a compiere ogni passo in piena autonomia. E' il 1973 quando nasce la *Grateful Dead Records*, etichetta destinata a produrre i dischi del gruppo, cui si aggiunge la *Round Records* per gli altri progetti. In proprio sono anche gli studi di registrazione *Le Club Front* a San Rafael e l'agenzia artistica che cura i tour, la *Fly by Night Travel*.

L'8 marzo 1973 la musica ha il suono sordo di un tonfo pallido e vuoto, Pig Pen muore nella sua casa di Corte Madera all'età di 27 anni. Sarà cremato così come voleva, vestito dell'amato giubbotto da motociclista, sulla sua lapide un epitaffio vero e sincero: *"Pig Pen é stato e ora sarà per sempre uno dei Grateful Dead"*. Con la morte di Pig Pen si chiude senza dubbio il capitolo iniziale della storia dei Grateful Dead. *History of the Grateful Dead (Volume One): Bear's Choice* é l'album di omaggio all'amico scomparso. Il brani del disco sono tratti dai concerti al Fillmore East del febbraio 1970 e la loro scelta é fatta da una vecchia conoscenza, Owsley, alias Bear. Particolarmente sanguigne risultano le versioni di *Hard to Handle*, *Smokestack Lightnin* e *Katie Mae*.

Il 28 luglio 1973 a Watkins Glenn, nei pressi di New York, si tiene il più grande concerto della storia del rock: oltre seicentomila persone assistono all'esibizione di Grateful Dead, Allman Brothers e The Band. Il ricordo stellare di quel giorno é la "Mountain Jam" degli Allman cui si aggiungono alcuni elementi dei Dead: grande e furioso il dialogo tra la chitarra di Garcia e quella di Dickey Betts. In ottobre esce l'album che tiene a battesimo la nuova etichetta: *Wake of the Flood* segna il ritorno in studio ed é finalmente un lavoro di un certo spessore.

The unfamiliarity with discographic moguls tied together with a natural bent to self management push the band to make a step toward the full automony. In 1973 the Grateful Dead Records is born, the new label who will produce the group's records together with its affiliated *Round Records* for external projects. Also the recording studios, the *Le Club Front* in San Rafael and the travel accomodation agency, the *Fly by Night Travel* were theirs.

On March 8, 1973, music gets the dumb sound of a pale and empty thud. Pig Pen dies in his home in Corte Madera aged 27. He has been buried has he wanted, dressed as a Hell's Angel, and on his gravestone a motto from the heart of the band: *"Pig Pen was and is now forever one of the Grateful Dead"*. The death of Pig Pen closes the first part of the story of the Grateful Dead.

History of the Grateful Dead (Volume one): Bear's Choice is the tribute record to the missing friend. All the tracks are from the *Fillmore East* concert in February 1970 and the choice has been made by a long time friend of the group, Bear, alias Owsley. Noteworthy are the versions of *Hard to handle, Smokestack lighnin'* and *Katie Mae*.

On July 28, 1973 at Watkins Glen, upstate New York, the biggest concert of the rock history is held. Well over 600.000 people attend the concert played by the *Grateful Dead*, the *Allman Brothers* and *The Band*. The stellar remembrance of that day is the "Mountain Jam" of the Allman Bros together with some of the Dead, with talking guitars of Garcia and Dickey Betts in an endless speech.

In October the record that christenize the new label: *Wake of the Flood* is released. It s the return of the Dead in the studio and is, at least, a good work.

Pig Pen

Al tempo stesso caldo e solare come in *Here Comes the Sunshine* e *Eyes of the World*, e poi decisamente malinconico come nella stupenda *Stella Blue* ed in *Weather Report Suite*.
Mississippi Half-Step Uptown Toodeloo e *Row Jimmy* sono le altre canzoni di valore dell'album che ha talvolta il difetto di essere appesantito dall'uso dei fiati.
Grateful Dead from the Mars Hotel è invece fatto di oro e carbone, vive di questo contrasto infatti l'album che esce nel giugno del 1974.
Tra le canzoni preziose come monete d'oro antico *Scarlet Begonias*, *Ship of Fools*, *China Doll* e *Unbroken chain* che vede cantare Lesh in studio per l'ultima volta. Affianco ad esse altre decisamente inutili come *Loose Lucy* e *Money Money*. Del disco fa parte anche l'ironica e rockeggiante *U.S. Blues*, futuro hit della band.
Sempre nel corso del 1974 giunge a termine un progetto da tempo coltivato, nasce il *Wall of Sound*, mega impianto di amplificazione. L'esordio è il 23 marzo '74 al Cow Palace di San Francisco e opportunamente lo show verrà battezzato *The Sound Test*.
L'incredibile struttura da 26.000 Watt verrà usata fino all'ottobre successivo, compreso il tour europeo, ma l'eccessivo costo di manutenzione e le difficoltà logistiche fanno sì che l'idea venga abbandonata.
La totale autogestione delle attività discografiche e concertistiche e la non prospera situazione economica cominciano intanto a pesare sul gruppo. Si prepara così una pausa di riposo e riflessione, tra il 16 ed il 20 ottobre 1974 i Grateful Dead tengono al Winterland i concerti di congedo dal loro pubblico. Nell'ultima serata si riunirà al gruppo Mickey Hart.
Gli shows vengono anche filmati per la realizzazione di un vecchio progetto di Garcia, un film che renda l'idea e lo spirito di un concerto dei Grateful Dead.
Verrà infatti poi tratto da questi filmati il *Dead Movie*, che vedrà la luce solo nel 1977.

The album has tracks with a warm sound like *Here comes sunshine* and *Eyes of the world*, then you can find some blue tracks like *Stella blue* or *Weather Report Suite*. The opening of *Mississippi Half-Step Uptown Toodeloo* with *Row Jimmy* are the other noteworthy songs of an album with the only flaws in the execssive use of the horns.
Grateful Dead from the Mars Hotel is a record made from gold and coal. Within these extremes lies the album released in June 1974.
Four are the songs precious like old works in gold: *Scarlet Begonias*, *Ship of fools*, *China doll* and *Unbroken Chain*, the latter with the last Phil Lesh vocals in recording studio, among other songs that are virtually useless like *Loose Lucy* and *Money money*. In the album we can find the ironical rocking *U.S. blues*, future hit by the band.
In 1974 a long time idea of the band, the *Wall of sound*, a mega-P.A, comes to an end. The maiden flight is on March 23, 1974 at the San Francisco's Cow Palace, and that show will be christened *The sound test*. The incredible bulding made of 26.000 watts will be used until October, including the european tour, but the excessive expenses and other difficulties bring the idea to a premature end.
The self management of both the record activities and live concert and bad financial status began to sink the band. In this way a hiatus is programmed in which the band could rest and reflect on its future.
From October 16 to 20, 1974, the Grateful Dead held at San Francisco's Winterland the "farewell concerts" to their fans.
On the last night Mickey Hart will reunite to the band. The shows had been shot for a future use in a major movie, an old idea of Garcia, a movie that will recreate the feeling and the spirit of a Grateful Dead concert.
This footage will take form as The *Dead Movie* in 1977.

Escono sempre nel corso del '74 i primi lavori della Round Records e cioé il secondo solo di Garcia, *Compliments*, e il disco d'esordio di Robert Hunter, *Tales of the Great Rum Runners*. Onestamente il disco di Garcia é una macchia nella carriera del 'maestro' mentre risulta decisamente felice il primo passo di Hunter.

La lunga pausa vede i membri della band impegnati in altri progetti. Garcia, insieme al tecnico del suono Dan Healy, passa buona parte del suo tempo lavorando all'editing del *Dead Movie*.

Esce intanto *Old & in the Way*, live registrato alla Boarding House di San Francisco nel corso del '73. All'epoca Garcia, insieme a vecchie conoscenze del bluegrass come Peter Rowan, Vassar Clements, David Grismann e John Kahn aveva dato vita all'omonima formazione. Tolto il banjo dalla soffitta e col cuore dei primi giorni nelle dita era nata questa avventura da piccolo club, il disco ne é degna testimonianza oltre che capolavoro nel suo genere.

Ma Garcia non é l'unico a muoversi, Bob Weir si esibisce col suo secondo gruppo, i *Kingfish*, mentre Phil Lesh lavora insieme a Ned Lagin, musicista e mago dell'elettronica, a un disco di pura sperimentazione, *Seastones*, cui collaborano anche David Crosby e Grace Slick.

Tuttavia il '75 non é completo vuoto siderale per migliaia di Deadheads orfani della band.

Il gruppo si esibisce come *Jerry Garcia & Friends* il 23 marzo 1975 per lo SNACK Benefit al Kezar Stadium di San Francisco.

Il concerto, a cui si uniscono anche *Ned Lagin* e *Merl Saunders*, é sicuramente uno dei più bizzarri in assoluto.

Il gruppo esegue un brano all'epoca in gestazione per il futuro disco, *Blues for Allah*, un percorso di dissonanze musicali lungo quaranta minuti cui segue una *Johnny B. Goode* al fulmicotone.

E' il 13 agosto 1975 quando i Grateful Dead fanno il loro rientro ufficiale esibendosi alla Great American Music Hall di San Francisco in occasione della première di *Blues for Allah*.

In 1974 see the first batch of Round Records releases: the Garcia second solo album, *Compliments*, and the first record by Robert Hunter, *Tales of the Great Run Runners*. The Garcia record is, honestly, a bad spot in the maestro's career, while the Hunter move is very good. The long pause sees the group's member busy on other projects. Garcia, together with the sound engineer Dan Healy, spent most of his time working on the editing of the *Dead Movie*. In the meantime *Old & in the Way*, a live recording made at the Boarding House in San Francisco in 1973 is released. At that time Garcia was playing with old bluegrass buddies like Peter Rowan, Vassar Clements, David Grismann, and with John Kahn they formed the eponymous group. Taken away the banjo from the garret and with the same heart as the first old days this adventure that fits small clubs, was born and the record is a genuine witness and a masterpiece in his genre. But Garcia is not the only one at the move, Bob Weir starts his second band, the *Kingfish*, while Phil Lesh works together with Ned Lagin, and experimental musician and electronic wizard, on a record of pure experimental sounds, called *Seastones* in which you could find David Crobsy and *Grace Slick*, too. 1975 is not completely empty for the thousands of Deadheads. The group will perform as Jerry Garcia and friends on March 23, 1975 at the SNACK benefit at the Kezar Stadium, San Francisco. The concert sees the band augmented by *Ned Lagin* and *Merl Saunders* and it is one of the strangest they ever played. The group performs a track then unknown that later surfaces on the new album *Blues for Allah*, a dissonant path long over forty minutes, then they play a furious *Johnny B. Goode* as encore. On August 13, 1975 the Grateful Dead return to the audience performing at the Great American Music Hall in San Francisco premiering the release of *Blues from Allah*.

Grateful Dead's lyricist Robert Hunter in front of the famous "Blues for Allah" cover

Per anni la potenza ed il feeling di questo concerto per pochi invitati - solo cinquecento persone - sono stati rinchiusi nei solchi del bootleg *Make Believe Ballroom*. Finalmente nel corso del 1991 arriverà la versione ufficiale della performance interamente riportata su *One from the Vault*. *Blues for Allah* é il tipico disco in studio dei Grateful Dead, fatto di luci e di ombre, si aggiunga poi in questo caso un misto di stili completamente diversi. Dagli spunti jazz d'apertura di *Help on the Way/Slipknot!* si passa al tipico suono Grateful Dead della favolosa *Franklin's Tower*, ci si tuffa nel ritmo sincopato di *The Music Never Stopped* e passando per la meravigliosa ballata che é *Crazy Fingers* si giunge agli arabeggianti pezzi finali, tra cui la title track. L'album *Steel your Face* é da molti ricordato solo per la bella copertina che sarà

For long years the power and the feeling of this concert for few - the audience was by special invitation for only 500 people - had been closed in the grooves of a bootleg record called *Make Believe Ballroom*. Finally 1991 sees the official release of this concert widely available on the double CD set *One from the Vaults*. *Blues for Allah* is the typical Grateful Dead studio album made of light and shadows, this time with added a mixture as different styles. From the jazz opening of *Help on the Way/Slipknot!* to the typical Grateful Dead sound of *Franklin's tower* and then to the syncopated rhythm of *The Music Never Stopped* landing on that wonderful slow ballad called *Crazy fingers* and ending on the arabian taste of the final tracks including the title track. The next record, *Steal your face* is remembered by many only for the cover that

The "Wall of sound", 1974. Grateful Dead with Keith & Donna Godchaux

poi motivo ricorrente nell'iconografia dei Grateful Dead. In effetti il doppio live, che si riferisce ai concerti del '74 al Winterland, vive nell'ombra tanto per la pessima qualità della registrazione quanto per l'assenza di nuove canzoni.

E' un gioco opaco, ed é anche l'ultimo disco per la Grateful Dead Records che chiude per le difficoltà economiche e manageriali.

Ma il 1976 é in parte riabilitato dal ritorno di Garcia al suo stile cristallino con il nuovo solo *Reflections*. Il disco è ricco di belle canzoni dalla poesia e linea melodica inappuntabili, *Comes a Time*, *Might as Well*, *Mission in the rain* e la dolcissima *It Must Have Been the Roses* su tutte. Esce anche *Diga*, il nuovo lavoro di *Mickey Hart* con la *Diga Rhytm Band*, formazione di percussionisti di varia scuola.

from then on will be a recurring pattern in the Grateful Dead iconography. The double live set comes from the farewell concerts of 1974 at Winterland and it is a record that is put in the shade both the lacking of new material and for the bad recording. This record is also the last of the Grateful Dead Records that shortly after closed down for economic and managerial difficulties. But 1976 sees also the return of Garcia on his "crystal style" on the guitar in his new solo record *Reflection*. The record is full of wonderful songs with excellent lyrics and unforgettable melodies, *Comes a time, Might as well, Mission in the rain* and over the top the sweetness of *It must have been the roses*. Round Records release *Diga*, the new work of Mickey Hart with the *Diga Rhythn Band*, a group made of percussionists only.

LET MY INSPIRATION FLOW

Chiusa la propria etichetta, i Grateful Dead sono corteggiati da molte case discografiche, alla fine firmano per la neonata *Arista Records* di Clive Davis, il quale assicura loro la completa libertà sul piano artistico. Si apre così sotto buoni auspici il 1977 nel corso del quale esce, in giugno, l'atteso *Dead Movie*. Il film é la memoria di spazi e terre felici, le canzoni, le immagini e il pubblico dei Deadheads sono testimoni dell'attimo in cui la musica diventa felicità. Il documento é unico anche per la spettacolare sequenza a cartoni animati che apre il filmato. Le animazioni realizzate da Gary Gutierez sono fuse in esatta simbiosi con i vari frammenti di canzoni e creano un paesaggio ironico e surreale nell'esatto simbolismo Grateful Dead.

Primo risultato per la nuova etichetta discografica é l'uscita di *Terrapin Station*. La suite che dà il titolo al disco é un capolavoro della penna visionaria di Robert Hunter e della melodia aurea di Jerry Garcia. Hunter scrive di getto il testo in una notte che avvolge San Francisco nella tempesta. La stessa notte Garcia sta tornando a casa in macchina, immerso nel temporale, con una melodia che gli mulina nel cervello. Il giorno dopo le parole incontrano la musica e così, da quella che sembra una favola della fantasia nasce una favola della realtà e il treno dei pensieri prende la strada della "Stazione di Terrapin". La versione del brano sul disco risulta, purtroppo, meno godibile di quella live. Le arbitrarie manipolazioni del produttore Keith Olsen in fase di mixaggio appesantiscono la struttura semplice e lineare della canzone. *Estimated Prophet*, della coppia Weir/Barlow, é l'altro pezzo chiave del nuovo vinile.

Nel luglio 1978 esce il disco più brutto in assoluto di tutta la carriera dei Grateful Dead. *Shakedown Street* é un episodio da dimenticare in fretta, fatta eccezione per due brani:

With the closing of their own record label the Dead were courted by several record companies, and in the end they will sign for the new born label of Clive Davis *Arista* which assure them the complete artistic freedom. With these omen the 1977 is born. In June the long awaited *Dead Movie* is released. The movie is the memory of free spaces and happy lands, the songs, the people of Deadheads all together witness the moment when music becomes happiness. This document is unique even for the cartoons that open the movie. The cartoons, created by Gary Gutierez, are melted together with the various songs painting an ironic and surrealistic landscape of the symbols of the Grateful Dead.

The first score for the new record label is the release of the album *Terrapin Station*. The suite that named the album is a truly masterpiece of the visionary pen of Robert Hunter and the golden melody of Jerry Garcia. Hunter recalls that he wrote all the lyrics in a night when a lightining storm was over San Francisco. In the same night, while coming home, Garcia is lost in the rain with a melody in his mind. The day after the words meet the music and, from what seems fantasy, a fairy tale of reality is born; the train of the mind is headed to *Terrapin Station*.

The recorded edition is, unfortunately, worst than the live one. The arbitrary adulteration of the producer (Keith Olsen) in the mixing makes the simply, almost linear, song structure heavy. *Estimated Prophet* by Weir/Barlow is the other kingpin of the album.

In July 1978 the worst record ever made by the Grateful Dead is released. *Shakedown Street* is an episode that we must forgive as soon as possible, except for two tracks, *Fire on the mountain* and *I need a miracle*.

Luckily 1978 will give the Dead and to their fans

Fire on the Mountain e *I Need a Miracle*. Fortunatamente il '78 regalerà ai Dead e ai propri fans due eventi indimenticabili. Tra il 14 e il 16 settembre hano luogo tre memorabili concerti al Sound & Light Theatre di Gizah, Egitto. Ai piedi della grande piramide si realizza un sogno coltivato da lungo tempo. La nuova situazione internazionale, figlia degli accordi di Camp David tra Carter, Begin e Sadat, fa cadere tutta una serie di veti e vincoli, creando un nuovo clima positivo da cui anche questa operazione trae beneficio. Musicalmente i tre concerti non sono tra i più belli, tanto é vero che tramonta subito l'idea di farne un disco. Tuttavia l'atmosfera magica e fantastica che circonda l'evento é veramente unica e tocca il culmine durante l'eclissi di luna che accompagna l'esibizione dell'ultima sera. Dall'America i Dead sono arrivati insieme ai vecchi amici e pionieri del sogno psichedelico, Ken Kesey, molti Pranksters, Owsley e l'inseparabile Bill Graham. L'altra punta di diamante dell'anno in corso é la chiusura del Winterland. Lo show per il New Year's Eve 1978/79 é una pietra miliare di tutta la storia concertistica dei Grateful Dead. Per la festa d'addio all'ultimo baluardo dei templi rock di San Francisco (il FillmoreWest aveva chiuso nel 1971) i Dead sfoderano una performance di incredibile bellezza e potenza. Nel corso della serata Matt Kelly, Lee Oskar, John Cipollina, Ken Kesey e i Merry Pranksters sono ospiti del concerto. Per Bill Graham e per il suo Winterland non poteva esserci festa migliore. La line-up del gruppo muta nei primi mesi del '79. Il 17 febbraio i coniugi Godchaux tengono il loro ultimo concerto, ed il successivo 22 aprile si unisce un nuovo tastierista, *Brent Mydland*, ex Silver e amico di Bob Weir. A guadagnarne in particolare sono le parti vocali, le fini armonie di Brent rsulteranno una delle carte vincenti degli anni '80. *Go to Heaven*, nuovo disco, esce ed apre la decade seguendo gli standards di studio.

two unforgettable events. Between September 14 and 16 the Grateful Dead held three concerts at the Gizah's "Sound & Light Theatre" in Egypt. At the foot of the great pyramid a long time dream comes true. The new world state, made by the "Camp David" agreement between Carter, Begin and Sadat, let some of the vetoes and bonds drop creating a positive situation from which this operation comes from. From the musical point of view these concerts are not among the best, so the idea of making a live recording is put apart soon. Neverthless the magic atmosphere of the event is unique and reaches its peak in the last concert, held while a lunar eclipse obscured the valley. From the US the Dead came together with longtime friends and pioneers of the psycehdelic dream, Ken Kesey, lots of Pranksters, Owsley and the inseparable Bill Graham.

The other gem of the year is the closing of Winterland. The New Year's Eve 1978/79 is a milestone of the entire concert history of the Grateful Dead. For the last party to the San Francisco's rock temple, (Fillmore West had closed down in 1971) the Dead come with a performance incredible both in beauty and in feeling. That night Matt Kelly, Lee Oskar, John Cipollina, Ken Kesey and the Merry Pranksters are guests. No one could imagine a better party for Bill Graham and his Winterland. The groups line-up change in the first months of 1979. On February 17 the Godchauxs play for the last time with the band on April 22 a new keyboard player is added to the group, *Brent Mydland*, ex *Silver* and Bob Weir's friend. The major gain is in the vocal parts, Brent fine armonies will be a winning card in the '80. *Go to Heaven*, the new record, is released and opens the decade following the studio standards. The best track is, undoubletly, *Althea*. Curious is the return of an old Standard *Don't ease me in*, first single of the group back in 1966.

Il pezzo forte é senza dubbio la love-ballad *Althea*. Una curiosità é data dal ritorno di *Don't Ease Me In*, primo singolo del gruppo targato 1966. Il 1980 segna anche il quindicesimo compleano della band, degnamente celebrato con due settimane di concerti al Warfield Theatre di San Francisco ed una al Radio City Music Hall di New York. Proprio da questi concerti del settembre/ottobre '80 nasceranno i due successivi live. *Reckoning* (aprile '81) é puro oro colato, musica incatenata al cielo sereno. Dopo circa dieci anni i Dead ripropongono un set completamente acustico e l'album in questione ne é la celebrazione ed il sorriso più luminoso. Lo stile inconfondibile del gruppo trabocca dai solchi e le raffinate armonie vocali marchiano col fuoco un viaggio attraverso i sentieri più puri della musica acustica americana. La sapiente miscela spazia tra classici di repertorio come *Dire Wolf, It Must Have Been the Roses, China Doll, Cassidy, Ripple* e traditionals come *Jack-a-Roe,Oh Babe Ain't No Lie, On the Road Again* e così via. Insomma, *Reckoning* é il disco da portarsi dietro il giorno del giudizio universale, da mostrare con orgoglio come un vestito nuovo. *Dead Set*, (agosto '81) é invece il lato elettrico. La potenza ed il ritmo diventano fuoco ardente per tutto lo scorrere del disco e la poesia dell'assolo di Garcia fa splendere di luce nuova vecchi classici da *Deal* a *Brokedown Palace*, da *Loser* alla furiosa versione di *Franklin's Tower*.

1980 marks the fifteenth anniversary of the band, that is celebrated with two full weeks of concerts at the San Francisco's Warfield Theatre and one week at the Radio City Music Hall in New York.
From these concerts of September/October the next two live records of the band are taken. *Reckoning* is released in April 1981 and is pure gold, music linked to the clear sky.
After almost ten years the Dead play again in acoustic set and this record is the celebration and the lightest smile.
The clearly recognizable style of the group overflows the grooves and the refined vocal armonies brand a trip through the purest paths of the american acoustic music.
The wise mixture varies to the group's own classics like *Dire Wolf, It must have been the roses, China Doll, Cassidy, Ripple*, and traditionals like *Jack-a-roe, Oh babe ain't no lie, On the road again* and so on.
Reckoning is the classic album to take along with you on the doomsday, to show with proudness like a new suit.
Dead set, released in August 1981, is the electric side of the new spring that the Grateful Dead are in.
The power and the rhythm becomes coal fire throughout the record, and the poetic solos of Garcia makes old classics like *Deal, Brokedown palace, Loser, Franklin's tower* shine with new light.

Dec. 31, 1978 - Closing of Winterland. With special guest John Cipollina

A TOUCH OF GRAY

Così la storia si ripete senza lasciare segni di stanchezza, i Grateful Dead proseguono instancabilmente la loro attività on the road, toccando nel corso dell'81 l'Europa per ben due volte. Delle due tournèes merita una notazione a parte il concerto di Essen, Germania, del 28 marzo 1981. La sua freschezza e passione, unite alla scelta dei brani ed alla magistrale esecuzione ne fanno un momento da conservare con indistruttibile gioia. Indimenticabile, nel cuore resterà l'assolo su *Sugaree*.
I concerti dei Dead sono un'interminabile festa itinerante per i sei anni che seguono e nel corso dei quali non vi sarà alcuna attività discografica. Solo concerti che toccano in lungo ed in largo gli States, una serie interminabile di sold-out che alimentano il mito di più grande 'concert-band' del mondo.
Ma ancora una volta giungono venti di gelo e l'ala della morte sembra in agguato. Dopo un paio di shows con Bob Dylan e Tom Petty, il 10 luglio 1986 Jerry Garcia cade in coma diabetico. Fortunatamente la lotta con la morte dura solo cinque giorni, ma quando Garcia si sveglia é costretto a ricominciare tutto da capo, parlare, camminare e ovviamente suonare. Il 15 Dicembre 1986 il grande ritorno all'Oakland Coliseum, una vera e propria ovazione accoglie le note di *Touch of Gray*, e quando Garcia intona *I will survive* la commozione é forte per il ritorno del vecchio amico.
Nel corso del 1987 i Dead tengono un mini-tour di sei date insieme a Bob Dylan: é da questi concerti che poi nel 1989 verrà realizzato l'album *Dylan & The Dead*. Ma la sorpresa che aspetta dietro l'angolo é grande, nel luglio dell'87 c'é l'atteso ritorno discografico. *In the Dark* é un buon disco che segna anche l'arrivo del successo commerciale, *Touch of Gray* entra infati nella top-ten dei singles in America.

As history repeat itself without signs of tireness, so the Grateful Dead keep on their untirable activity on the road landing in Europe for two times in 1981.
The noteworthy of the two is the first, for the Essen, Germany, concert of March 28. Its freshness and passion added to the happy choice of the songs and the perfect rendition makes this concert something to be conserved with unlimited joy. If we must choose something from that night, the part that we will carry in our heart is the guitar solo in one of the best *Sugaree* ever.
The live concert of the Grateful Dead became a moving party for the next six years and they didn't release any new record in the meanwhile.
Only concert from one side to the other of the States, long series of sold out that feed the myth of the biggest "concert-band" of the world.
Once again chilly winds came and the wing of the death is very near.
After a couple of shows with Bob Dylan and Tom Petty, on July 10, 1986, Jerry Garcia falls in diabetic come. Luckily the struggle for death lasted only five days, but when he awoke he had to face a different situation: he had to learn everything again, talk, walk, and play.
On December 15, 1986 is the big comeback at the Oakland Coliseum, a real standing ovation greets the notes of *Touch of gray*, and when Garcia sung *I will survive* the commotion's getting a high point for the old friend return.
In 1987 the Dead held a mini-tour of six dates only with Bob Dylan, and from these concerts in 1989 will be produced *Dylan & The Dead*.
But the big surprise is in waiting and July sees the release of the new studio album.
In the Dark is a good record that marks even the arrival of big money, *Touch of gray* is in the top ten in the US.

Ma anche altri brani si guadagnano una medaglia sul campo, *Throwing Stones* che é l'urlo di Weir contro la pazzia della guerra, e la celestiale ballata a firma Garcia/Hunter che é *Black Muddy River*. Esce nell'ottobre dello stesso anno anche *So Far*, video realizzato da Garcia e Lenn Dell'Amico. Le immagini sono decisamente oniriche e suggestive ed il grande lavoro al computer graphic aggiunge alla musica una spazialità superba.

Sulla scia del precedente arriva alla fine dell'89 *Built to Last*, disco che forse strizza un pò troppo l'occhio al dollaro. Nonostante lo sposalizio commerciale ci sono diverse canzoni dalla memoria forte e chiara dei giorni migliori. Così infatti per la title track, *Victim or the Crime* e *Standing on the Moon*, diamante che viene fuori dalle mani di Garcia.

Tra gli altri un brano di Mydland dal sapore profetico, *I Will Take You Home*.

Other tracks are worthwhile too, *Throwing stones*, the Bob Weir's cry against the madness of the war, and the celestial ballad signed Garcia/Hunter named *Black muddy river*. In the same year, but in October, *So Far* is released, a video realized by Garcia e Lenn Dell'Amico. The images are surely oneiric and the great work in computer graphic add to the Dead's music a superb spatiality.

On the track of the previous album at the end of 1989 comes *Built to last*, a record that blinkes too much to the top ten. Although not strong as the others this album has some of the songs with the clear and strong memory of better days. In this way the title track, *Victim of the crime* and *Standing on the Moon*; the latter is the diamond carved from Garcia's hands. In the record, among others, there's a track by Brent Mydland that has a prophetic flavour, *I will take you home*.

Brent Mydland

La luce pallida della morte si porta via Brent il 26 luglio 1990, e purtroppo l'amarezza é doppia essendo la causa un'overdose. Come per Pig Pen e Keith Godchaux una maledizione sembra perseguitare i tastieristi dei Grateful Dead. Con Brent il gruppo perde un ottimo musicista ed un eccellente vocalist. A sostituirlo arriva *Vince Welnick*, ex *Tubes*, cui si aggiunge spesso in concerto *Bruce Hornsby*, con il suo tocco di piano.

Esce intanto *Without a Net*, triplo live che celebra i venticinque anni di attività. Il suono di quest'album é quanto di più puro i Dead siano riusciti a catturare dal vivo. In particolare la chitarra di Garcia snocciola una dopo l'altra note che non sono suoni ma schegge di limpida purezza. Il disco si chiude con un inedito di grande suggestione: *Dear Mr. Fantasy* degli indimenticabili Traffic.

Parte con la nuova formazione ed a supporto del disco la festa per le nozze d'argento della band che ha il suo apice nel tour europeo dell'autunno 1990. Dopo nove lunghi anni il popolo d'Europa ha nuovamente il piacere di riabbracciare un sogno troppo diviso da un oceano, ed é un successo travolgente da Stoccolma a Berlino, da Parigi a Londra.

Il 1991 si segnala per due novità discografiche. Agli inizi dell'anno esce il già citato *One from the Vault*, primo figlio di una operazione che mira a 'tirar fuori dalla cantina' le migliori performances del gruppo.

Infrared Roses esce nel dicembre 1991. E' allo stesso tempo un disco bello e difficile, nessuna canzone ma solo intermezzi dalle jams e dai drums che puntuali si presentano ad ogni concerto.

Il risultato ci dice come i Dead e la loro musica siano un'entità in movimento, la sperimentazione prosegue verso territori sonori inesplorati.

Il 1992 é oggi e il viaggio ormai per noi é quasi in diretta.

The pale light of death will carry away Brent on July 26, 1990, and the bitterness is doubled as brought by an overdose.
Like Pig Pen and Keith Godchaux a curse seems cast over the Dead keyboard players.
The lost of Brent is not only for an excellent musician and extraordinairy vocalist, but most of all for a friend.
The new keyboard player will be *Vince Welnick*, from the *Tubes*, and in concert *Bruce Hornsby* will add his magical touch on piano.
In the same time *Without a net*, a triple album set recorded live is released.
The album celebrates the twenty five years of activity of the band. The sound is the purest the Dead had ever caught live.
Particularly the Garcia's guitar plays one after the others notes that don't seems sounds but crystal clear diamonds.
The album closes with a unreleased track full of suggestion, *Dear mr. Fantasy* of *Traffic* memories.
With the new line up and supporting the record the party for the silver wedding began.
The high point of this party is fall european tour of 1990. After nine long years europeans have once again the pleasure to embrace a dream.
Success is overwhelming from Stokholm to Berlin, from Paris to London.
1991 sees the release of two different records.
In the first part of the year *One from the Vaults* sees the light of the day; first son of an operation that "takes from the archives" the group best performances.
Infrared roses in December is a good record but also a hard one, as it is made of no songs, but only of extracts of the live jams of the second part of every concert.
The results show how the Dead and their music are a moving entity, with the experiment heading toward new territories.
1992 is now and the trip is almost a sync broadcast.

Ultimo figlio che arriva col vento della sera é *Two from the Vault*, episodio che segna la seconda tappa di una ricerca tra i tesori conservati negli archivi dei Dead. Dalla cantina arriva un'esplosione lunga due ore di musica e di ricordi, l'emozione ed il canto suonano come la campana che annuncia il nuovo giorno. Il concerto che ci viene consegnato é infatti del lontano '68 e da allora di giorni ne verranno, tanti, luminosi ed indimenticabili. In questo disco torna anche il mai dimenticato Pig Pen, che forse é davvero lì da qualche parte che guarda, ascolta, sorride e canta, a modo suo, come sempre e come questo disco testimonia. Sulla riva del Pacifico soffia oggi un vento che porta nuovi profumi, ci sono quattro nuove canzoni che i Dead stanno presentando nei loro concerti più recenti: *Way to Go Home* di Vince Welnick, *Wave to the Wind* di Phil Lesh, *Corinna* di Bob Weir e *So Many Roads* di Jerry Garcia. Abbiamo avuto modo di sentirle e possiamo solo aspettarci cose buone, in particolare Garcia sembra aver scoperto il moto perpetuo della dolcezza.
Aspettiamo così il nuovo album, aspettiamo che l'autobus passi nuovamente da queste parti e ci carichi su ancora una volta, in compagnia di questa vecchia storia americana fatta di amore e di musica. La leggenda continua ed é iscritta nell'angolo migliore del cuore.

The last son, the one that comes with night wind, is *Two from the vaults*, the new episode that marks the second lap in a search of treasures kept in the Dead's archives.
From that basement a blast of two full hours comes, mixed with music and remembrances, the emotions and the songs are the chimes of the new day.
The concert, as a matter of fact, is from the long passed 1968 and from that day on many, enlighting and unforgettables days to come. In this record we find again the never forgotten Pig Pen, that is looking here smiling and singing, in his way, like always, and this record is the testimonial.
On the Pacific shore a new wind blows today, bringing new smells. There are four new songs that the Dead are playing.
These are *Way to go home*, by Vince Welnick, *Wave to the wind* by Phil Lesh, *Corinna* by Bob Weir and *So many roads* by Jerry Garcia.
We had the pleasure to listen to all of them and we are waiting for good things, expecially from the Garcia's one, that seems to have discovered the secret of the perpetual mote of sweetness.
We are waiting for the new album, and for the bus to pass once again, in good company of this american history made of love and music.
The legend continues and is written in the best part of our heart.

Grateful Dead & Bob Dylan, 1987

JERRY GARCIA
THE GURU

Jerry Garcia, the lead guitarist and central figure of The Grateful Dead, has been a musical guru to an entire generation of San Francisco musicians. Just as the Dead's first album was about to be released, this interview was done with him. It is, in several ways, indicative of the roots, the aspirations and influences of San Francisco music.
The Dead, like the Airplane, are still intact, the originals and still champions of what we have to come to know as the adult rock sound.

Being in a recording situation is really a lot different than playing. A recording situation brings out a special, sort of like another side of creativity. It's something like painting or drawing or anything that you do over a long period of time for a finished product. And so when you get into a recording studio you begin to have a different feeling about what you're doing. And that's something we're just starting to get into too. So the first album was essentially a live album. They were going to put that really ostentatious oriental quotation, "Egyptian Book of the Dead" quotation on the top but we...

Is that where the name Grateful Dead comes from?

No, it doesn't, as a matter of fact. It came out of a big Webster's dictionary or a New World or an Oxford dictionary. Just opened it and there it was. Just happened to turn to a page that had Grateful Dead on it.
When we were looking for a name.

Where did you get the tunes on the first album from?

They came from a lot of different places. Like on the album, the material comes from blues, like some of the material is from blues, recent blues, like the last ten years' blues.

Jerry Garcia, la chitarra solista e figura centrale dei Grateful Dead, é stato un guru musicale per un'intera generazione di musicisti di San Francisco. L'intervista ha avuto luogo proprio quando il primo album dei Dead stava per essere messo in commercio ed è, per molti versi, indicativa delle radici, delle aspirazioni e delle influenze della scena musicale di San Francisco. I Dead, come gli Airplane, sono ancora gli stessi, originali campioni, di quel che abbiamo conosciuto come rock adulto.

Dover registrare delle cose è davvero molto diverso dal suonare. Una registrazione porta fuori qualcosa di speciale, come un'altra parte della creatività. E' qualcosa di simile al dipingere o disegnare o qualcos'altro tu debba fare per un lungo periodo di tempo per arrivare al prodotto finale. E così quando entri in uno studio di registrazione inizi ad avere sensazioni diverse su quel che stai facendo. E questo per noi é qualcosa che é solo agli inizi. Per questo il primo album é essenzialmente un album dal vivo. Avrebbero voluto mettere quella stentata citazione orientale "Il libro egiziano dei morti" in cima ma noi...

Ed é da lì che vi é venuta l'idea del nome Grateful Dead?

No, non é così, é un dato di fatto. Viene da un grosso dizionario Webster, o da un New World, o da un dizionario Oxford. L'abbiamo aperto e ce lo siamo trovati lì. E' solo successo che abbiamo girato una pagina che iniziava con Grateful Dead quando eravamo in cerca di un nome.

Da dove avete preso le canzoni per il primo album?

Da tante parti diverse. Come sull'album, il materiale viene dal blues, tutto un pò del materiale é dal blues, blues recente, quello degli ultimi dieci anni. Il blues di Chicago.

Chicago style blues.Like *Good morning little schoolgirl* is a song that's in the public domain and we left it in the public domain, by the way, we didn't copyright any of this shit, the stuff that's traditional we left traditional. *Good morning little schoolgirl* is a traditional song but it's only as far as I know maybe 10, 15 years old. Not much older than that. Some of the others are much older. *Cold rain and snow* is a fragment that I learned from a banjo player named Obray Ramsey. A traditional singer from someplace like Indiana. It's in the same kind of mode as it originally was but the melody is different. And we've added a harmony line and of course it's us, it's our rhytmic structure and our ideas. *Sittin' on the top of the world* is another traditional song that was copyrighted some time not too long ago by some country and western guy but it's still essentially a folk song. There are just two or three verses and they're standard blues verses that turn up everywhere. And again, that's our arrangement...

Prendi *Good morning little schoolgirl*, é una canzone di dominio pubblico ed é così che noi l'abbiamo lasciata, non abbiamo messo niente di tutta questa robaccia sotto copyright, quel che é tradizionale lasciamo che resti tradizionale. E *Good morning little schoolgirl* è una canzone tradizionale pur avendo solo 10, 15 anni. Non più vecchia di tanto. Altre ancora sono molto più vecchie. *Cold rain and snow* é un frammento che ho appreso da un suonatore di banjo: Obray Ramsey. Un cantante tradizionale di qualche posto tipo l'Indiana. E' rimasta com'era ma é cambiata la melodia. Certo vi abbiamo aggiunto una diversa linea armonica e le nostre idee. *Sittin' on the top of the world* é un'altra canzone tradizionale messa sotto coopyright non molto tempo fa da un tizio che fa country & western pur essendo essenzialmente una canzone folk. Ci sono solo due o tre versi che sono poi quelli classici del blues. Ancora una volta, quello é il nostro arrangiamento...

Grateful Dead, 1966

Most of these things, that we've done is we've taken an idea and just developed it. *Viola Lee Blues*, the long one on the album, it's about 10 minutes or 11 minutes or something like that. And the words to that and a certain amount of the phrasing, the way the words are sung, comes from a record by Noah Lewis who used to be the harmonica player in Gus Cannon and His Jug Stompers. Really beautiful lyrical harmonica player, one of the early guys. And this song, a good example of how it used to go when Noah Lewis had it, was the Jim Kweskin Jug Band, they do it almost the same way Noah Lewis does it in terms of the way they sing it. Our way is quite a lot jazzier and it has a newer rhytm and we've also done some things with the bar lengths in it. We've slipped in a half bar where there would normally be a bar. It's sort of like a 12-bar blues but in this case it's 11 and half-bar blues, 'cause we left out a half bar to make the phrasing ant the background work together. It's pretty interesting. And then of course, we will like improvise with it for a long time and do a lot of things in it. Again it's a framework more than anything else. But the words are real powerful, simple direct things.

11 and half, 11 and half, 11 and half?

Yeah, right. It goes 11 and half, 11 and half, 11 and half. We also, the way we play our stuff is if we're using changes, like blues changes, we frequently throw in two or three bars of just 'comping before getting into the changes. Or sometimes we eliminate the changes entirely.

So the construction of the thing, if you were to write it out, is asymmetrical. It's not ever *quite* 11 and half bars and it's not ever a straight 12 bars either. It instead has added bars here and there and tags and so forth.

That's the thing that occurs in traditional music and doesn't occur too much in more formalized kinds of music.

Nella maggior parte di questi casi, tutto quello che abbiamo fatto é stato prendere un'idea e svilupparla. *Viola Lee Blues*, quella lunga nel disco, dura circa 10 o 11 minuti, o qualcosa del genere. Le parole, qualche frase, il modo in cui vengono cantate sono prese da un disco di Noah Lewis, l'armonicista di Gus Cannon e i suoi Jug Stompers. Davvero un meraviglioso suonatore d'armonica, uno di quei tipi primordiali. Un buon esempio di come questo pezzo dovesse andara ci viene dalla Jim Kwesin Jug Band che lo faceva quasi come Noah Lewis per quanto riguarda il modo di cantare. Noi la facciamo un pò più jazzata, con un ritmo nuovo ed una durata diversa. Abbiamo accelerato di mezza battuta dove normalmente ci stava una battuta. E' come un blues in dodici battute, ma in questo caso é un blues in 11 battute e mezza, percé abbiamo lasciato fuori mezza battuta per lasciare che il fraseggio ed il sottofondo potessero funzionare insieme. E' molto interessante. E poi, ovviamente, ci piace improvvisare e farci un sacco di cose.

Ancora una volta é più un frammento che altro. Ma le parole dono davvero potenti, cose semplici e dirette.

11 e mezzo, undici e mezzo, undici e mezzo?

Sì, giusto, va in undici e mezzo, undici e mezzo, undici e mezzo. Abbiamo anche un modo tutto nostro di suonare i pezzi e se usiamo dei cambi, come per il blues, ci mettiamo spesso due o tre battute di sola attesa prima dell'entrata dei cambi stessi. O altre volte questi cambi li eliminiamo del tutto. Così costruiamo le cose, in maniera, se vuoi scriverlo, asimmetrica. Non é sempre con battute da 11 e mezzo ma neanche con le canoniche 12 battute. Al loro posto abbiamo aggiunto battute qui e là, altrove seguito fedelmente e così via. Questo é quel che succede nella musica tradizionale mentre non capita spesso nelle forme più istituzionalizzate.

Now, when you play it, do you play it the same way all the time?

No, never.

Do you change that structure?

Always. That's the part that's fun about it, because it's like we all have to be on our toes. All of a sudden there's something new entering and we all try and pick up on it. That's when we're playing good; if we're not playing good that doesn't happen. But you know about that, you know. Like sometimes you can do it and sometimes you can't. And in this case, the way we did this was interesting. Each night when we went into the studio we played *Viola Lee Blues*. For as long as we wanted to play it and we recorded it. And then at the end of the week we went through them and listened to them and the one that turned us on was the one. So that's the one we used. The one that turned us on. It isn't good as it *could* have been but it's still okay. It's still okay. It's always like after the fact of the recording I don't want to say too much about it, it's like it's finished and it's sort of in the past.
And none of the material we're doing that's on the record is going to be much like the record from now on. Because now we feel we've done it that way. I'm even thinking perhaps there's a possibility of re-recording some of this stuff sometime in the future just for the sake of how much it's changed. I'll have to explain about the four or five idioms that we work in and our music is more or less idiomatic and we do material for the way it is and the way we are kind of comes out through.
Do you know what I mean?
So our arrangements differ from song to song and our ideas differ, but because of the way we approach our individual instruments, our individual styles can be picked out.
Our way of playing. It's hard to like... I'd say that we'd stolen freely from everywhere! Remorselessly and freely!

Ma, quando eseguite il brano, lo suonate sempre alla stessa maniera?

No, mai.

Nel senso che cambiate la struttura?

Sempre. Questo é il bello, ciò che rende la faccenda interessante. D'improvviso c'é qualcosa di nuovo che entra: la prendiamo al volo e la proviamo tutti. Quando suoniamo bene. Se non stiamo suonando bene non succede niente di tutto questo. Ma sai già come vanno queste cose, lo sai. A volte lo puoi fare ed altre no. In questo caso ci é sembrato interessante come l'abbiamo fatto. Ogni sera che entravamo in studio facevamo *Viola Lee Blues*, per tutto il tempo che volevamo, poi l'abbiamo registrata. Finita la settimana abbiamo preso tutte le versioni e, ascoltandole, ci siamo accorti che la migliore era la prima, quella che ci ha colpiti di più. Non é così buona come avrebbe potuto essere ma va bene così. Va ancora bene. E' sempre la storia della registrazione, non voglio farla tanto lunga, una volta finita é come se appartenesse al passato. E niente del materiale che facciamo e che é sul disco sarà come é stato inciso, da ora in poi. Perché adesso sentiamo di averla fatta in quel determinato modo. A volte penso alla possibilità di ri-registrare qualcosa in futuro solo per rimarcare le cose che sono cambiate.
Vorrei dire qualcosa in merito ai quattro o cinque idiomi che usiamo per lavorare: la nostra musica é più o meno idiomatica e noi lavoriamo sui pezzi per quello che sono e per quel che noi pensiamo possa venirne fuori. Capisci quel che voglio dire? Così i nostri arrangiamenti variano da canzone a canzone ed é così anche per le nostre idee, dipende dall'approccio ai singoli strumenti, dallo stile individuale in cui possono essere suonati. Il nostro modo di suonare. E' difficile, é come... vorrei dire che abbiamo preso liberamente da qualsiasi posto! Liberamente e senza alcun rimorso!

Our ideas come from everywhere, and we have no bones about mixing our idioms or throwing stuff back and forth from one place to another. So you might hear some very straight traditional counterpoint, classical-style counterpoint popping up in the middle of some rowdy thing. And just because we do whatever is fun or whatever is exciting for us musically.

Le nostre idee vengono da ogni parte e non ci facciamo problemi nel mischiare i nostri linguaggi o nel buttar via delle cose saltando da un posto all'altro. Puoi sentire qualche contrappunto alla maniera più tradizionale, o qualcosa in stile classico che salta fuori nel bel mezzo di qualcosa di grezzo. E quel che musicalmente ci eccita è proprio il fare quel che più ci piace.

Grateful Dead, 1966

Do you come from diverse musical backgrounds?

Oh, yes. Diverse isn't the word for it! Like my background in music...
My first guitar was an electric guitar and my first love on the guitar was Chuck Berry.
He was my guy. When I was a kid I got all his records and I'd just try like crazy to learn how to play them.
I got this electric guitar and I didn't know anything about the guitar.
I had the guitar for maybe six or eight months without ever knowing how to tune it and I invented a tuning for it and invented a way to play it in this tuning so it worked out pretty well until I got to certain points.
I'd listen to a record and I'd try to figure out what the guy was doing and it was virtually impossible to do because of the way I had my guitar tuned! Finally I ran into a guy who showed me how to tune it; he showed me a few of the basic chords and it was just a revelation!
Here it was! The real way to do it!
So I went for a while into rock'n'roll, like About two years perhaps and I played more or less unsuccessfully with a few little two-saxophone-and-piano bands and electric guitar and amplifier about this big. Little pea shooter of an amplifier.
And then my next change in music was when the whole folk-music thing started happening.
And I got caught up into that... I got listening to... when Joan Baez's first record came out I heard it and I heard her finger picking the guitar, I'd never heard anything like it before so I got into that and I started getting into country music, into old time white music.
Mostly white spiritual stuff, white instrumental music and I got into finger style, the folk-music-festival scene, that whole thing.
And I was very heavy into that for a long time and I sort of employed a scholarly approach and even went through the South with tape recorders and stuff recording blue-grass bands.

Venite da diversi retroterra musicali?

Oh, sì. Diversi non é la parola giusta! Come il mio retroterra musicale... La mia prima chitarra era una chitarra elettrica ed il mio primo amore alla chitarra fu Chuck Berry.
Lui era il mio tipo. Quand'ero ragazzo avevo tutti i suoi dischi e diventavo pazzo per cercare di imparare a suonare i suoi pezzi. Avevo questa chitarra elettrica e non sapevo un accidente in merito allo strumento. Passarono sei o otto mesi senza che io nemmeno sapessi come accordarla, tanto che avevo inventato un sistema di accordatura ed un modo di suonare con questa accordatura, e questo funzionava fino ad un certo punto. Ascoltavo un disco e cercavo di capire cosa stesse facendo il tipo, ma mi risultava praticamente impossibile per la maniera in cui la mia chitarra era accordata!
Finalmente trovai uno che mi fece vedere come si faceva ad accordarla, insegnandomi qualche accordo di base: fu una rivelazione!
Ecco! Così si fa! E così mi diedi per un pò al rock'n'roll, per circa due anni forse. Ho anche suonato con scarso successo con qualche piccolo gruppo da due sassofoni e un piano con una chitarra elettrica ed un amplificatore grosso così. Una piccola cerbottana di amplificatore. Il mio successivo cambiamento musicale avvenne allorché l'intera scena folk cominciò a venire fuori. Ci finii dentro... cominciai ad ascoltare queste cose... quando uscì il primo disco di Joan Baez lo ascoltavo e sentivo le sue dita che toccavano la chitarra, non avevo mai sentito nulla di simile prima così cominciai ad interessarmi di queste cose arrivando al country, alla musica bianca tradizionale. Perlopiù spiritual bianchi, musica bianca strumentale; mi diedi all'arpeggio, alla scena dei folk festivals, a tutte queste cose. Ci rimasi per molto tempo, con convinzione. Un approccio di tipo scolastico che mi portò nel Sud con tanto di registratore per registrare i gruppi di blue-grass.

I spent about three years playing blue-grass banjo, that was my big thing and I almost forgot how to play the guitar during that period of time. And then I got into a jug band, we got a jug band going and I took up the guitar again and from the jug band it was right into rock'n'roll. And so like my background is essentially very straight musically. The traditional forms of music are mostly musically direct. They have simple changes and simple ideas and the melodic lines are easy and so forth but they have a lot of... the interest is in the form, you know, and like the fine points of the form like flamenco guitar or something...

You didn't study anywhere?

No, just on my own, books and whatever, you know, records. And listened a lot and played a lot. That was about all it amounted to.
Phil, our bass player, is the one who has the longest thing in music. He's been in music for about 20 years. He started off playing violin, classical violin and then he played trumpet. And he played trumpet in the San Mateo College Band, the jazz band. And he wrote a lot of arrangements for them too. Stan Kenton-style arrangements. He played those screechy Maynard Ferguson parts, pass out on the stage! And then he got into more modern music, like through jazz. He was also always interested in classical all through this time. He got into modern forms of music, serial music and 12-tone music, 12-tone composition and finally electronic music and he composed these monster things. He has absolute pitch. He used to like over in Berkeley, I'd come over and he'd have these monster pieces of score paper and he'd be working away, working in pen, the notes are coming out of his head, out on to the paper! These things for like 12 orchestras and whatever!
And the big problem, of course, when you're a serious composer is getting anybody to play your stuff; it's virtually impossible. A young composer? No way!

Ho passato circa tre anni a suonare il banjo bluegrass, il mio interesse principale che quasi mi aveva fatto dimenticare come si suonasse la chitarra. Poi é stata la volta di una jug band, dove ho imbracciato di nuovo la chitarra e dalla jug band dritto al rock'n'roll. Un retroterra musicale piuttosto normale.
Le forme tradizionali di musica sono musicalmente le più dirette. Hanno semplici stacchi e semplici idee, con le linee melodiche facili e così via, il fatto é che hanno... l'interessante é nella forma, capisci, nelle rifiniture della forma come per la chitarra flamenco e queste cose...

Non hai studiato da qualche parte?

No, ho fatto tutto da solo, libri e tutto quanto, voglio dire, dischi. Ascoltando e suonando molto. E' così che sono cresciute le cose.
Phil, il nostro bassista, é quello che la sa più lunga di musica. Ci é stato dentro per almeno 20 anni. Ha cominciato suonando il violino e poi la tromba. Suonava la tromba nella College Band di San Mateo, la jazz band. Ha scritto anche un sacco di arrangiamenti per loro, tipo Stan Kenton. Suonava quelle stridenti parti alla Maynard Ferguson, da svenire sul palco! Poi é passato alla musica moderna, magari attraverso il jazz. Ai tempi era molto interessato alle cose classiche. Cominciò ad interessarsi delle forme più innovative, musica seriale e dodecafonica, composizioni dodecafoniche ed infine musica elettronica, fino a comporre cose davvero imponenti.
Un tocco tutto suo. Se ne stava a Berkeley, io andavo lì e lui aveva questi pezzi pazzeschi di carta che riutilizzava per lavorarci con la penna, le note gli uscivano dalla testa direttamente sulla carta!
Roba tipo 12 orchestre e cose del genere!
Il vero problema, ovviamente, quando sei un compositore serio, é trovare qualcuno che esegua il tuo materiale, che é virtualmente impossibile. Un giovane compositore? Non c'é verso!

So he studied with Berio over at Mills for a long time and then, the way he describes it is, he suddenly found himself out of that. I mean it was just like he had gone as far as he could go in his own head with that. And he just stopped doing it and he was doing nothing for a while and then he went to see the Beatles! The Beatles movie came out about that time.

He went to see the Beatles and it of course blew his mind and he grew his hair long and started going to the early dances.

When The Byrds were playing in town and all that was just starting to happen. And he and I had been friends for a long time. He used to work at KPFA, he once recorded me in a folk-music show and he and I had been getting stoned together for years and scheming and plotting but we'd never gotten together musically. We were mutual admirers.

And at that time I was just finished with the jug band, just starting the rock'n'roll band, we had this other bass player, and I talked to Phil.

And he said he'd like to take it up so I showed him a few things, two weeks later we played our first job! Him playing bass for two weeks! Never played a fretted instrument before, but his mind is so incredibly musical. So that's his background. He's incredible, really musically articulate.He knows more about music than almost anybody I know, he's fantastic.

Pigpen, his father was the first rhytm and blues guy around here, you know. And he's always heard blues since he was a tiny kid and he played piano for a long time, just simple C blues runs and stuff like that and he'd sing.

When I met him, he was about 14 or 15. And he was already a step removed from school and family and everything like that and he was hanging around at the various scenes that were going on in Palo Alto at that time.

At that time I was sort of a beatnik guitar player. And he'd come around to these parties and I'd be playing blues and he'd watch very carefully and he'd go home and learn things, all on the sly.

Così ha cominciato a studiare con Berio a Mills per un lungo periodo e poi, così dice lui, si trovò a non avere più interessi in questo campo. Forse aveva raggiunto la massima espansione che poteva avere la sua testa in queste cose. Smise dunque di interessarvisi e rimase per un pò senza far niente di particolare finché non andò a vedere i Beatles! Il film sui Beatles uscì proprio in quei momenti. La vista dei Beatles gli diede naturalmente una bella scossa e così si lasciò crescere i capelli e ad andare ai primi balli. Quando i Byrds suonavano in città e tutto quanto stava cominciando a succedere. Lui ed io eravamo stati amici per lungo tempo. Lui lavorava alla KPFA e una volta aveva registrato un mio spettacolo di folk music e avevamo sballato insieme per anni cercando di programmare una qualche maniera di lavoro comune in campo musicale. Ci ammiravamo vicendevolmente. Erano i tempi in cui avevo quasi finito con la jug band per dare inizio al gruppo di rock'n'roll, avevamo quest'altro bassista e ne parlai a Phil. Per lui andava bene e gli mostrai alcune cose: due settimane dopo il nostro primo ingaggio! Aveva suonato il basso per sole due settimane! Mai suonato prima uno strumento coi tasti, ma la sua mentalità e così incredibilmente musicale. E questo é il suo background. E' incredibile, davvero articolato musicalmente.

Lui sa di musica più di qualsiasi altro che conosca, é fantastico.

Pigpen, suo padre fu il primo ad interessarsi di rhytm and blues da queste parti, capisci.

E così ha sempre sentito il blues sin da quando era piccolo, ha suonato il piano a lungo, semplici blues in Do e roba simile, cantando pure.

Quando l'ho incontrato, aveva circa 14 o 15 anni. Si era già allontanato da scuola e dalla famiglia per girare attorno alle varie scene che stavano allora facendosi avanti a Palo Alto.

A quei tempi io ero una specie di suonatore di chitarra beatnik. Lui veniva a queste feste dove io suonavo del blues, guardava attentamente e andava a casa a cercare di imparare di nascosto.

And he took up harmonica as well, back in those days and one day he'd been playing harmonica for a long time, he was deathly afraid to play in front of anybody, he'd been playing harmonica secretly, and one time he got up on stage at a folk-music place and I backed him up on the guitar; he played harmonica and sang. And he could sing like Lightnin' Hopkins, which just like blew everybody's mind! Here he was, 15 years old with this shaky voice and all this stuff and he could like improvise endlessly. Just endlessly! He could just make up millions and millions of verses that were all just fantastic and he's really the master at the shady comment in blues, the blues scene. Whatever it is, really a sort of a complicated thing, but he's into that heavier than anybody I know. And so like his thing is blues, almost nothing but blues, he's got some interest in other kind of music, but it's mostly blues. Like he listens to Jimmy Smith more on the organ than anybody else. And he's only been playing the organ as long as the band's been together. He doesn't really work at it too hard, not as hard as the rest of us do for example, but he has a good mind for phrasing, he's got real clear ideas. And he's always got a way, he can always make a song nicer by the thing that he plays. He's a real great supporting organist. He hasn't got a real heavy chord background or anything like that but he's got a good mind for lines.

And so that's Pigpen.

Aveva anche un'armonica , una volta l'ha suonata per tanto tempo, ma aveva una paura mortale di suonare di fronte a chiunque, se la suonava in segreto e una volta salì sul palco in un locale folk dove l'accompagnavo alla chitarra: suonava l'armonica e cantava. Poteva cantare come Lightnin' Hopkins facendo andare tutti fuori di testa! Era così, 15 anni e questa voce che ti scuoteva e tutte queste cose e poteva improvvisare all'infinito. Proprio all'infinito! Poteva eseguire mille e mille strofe e tutto questo era semplicemente fantastico. Lui è davvero maestro dei blues più oscuri, della scena blues. Di qualunque cosa si tratti, é comunque una faccenda complicata, ma lui é dentro questa storia più pesantemente di chiunque altro io conosca. Anche perché questo é il blues, nient'altro che blues, si, ha avuto anche altri interessi in altri generi, ma più che altro blues. Come ascoltare Jimmy Smith all'organo di chiunque altro. Ha suonato solamente l'organo finchè la band non si é messa assieme. Non gli va di lavorare troppo duramente, non tanto come al resto di noi, per esempio, ma ha una buona testa per il fraseggio, ha delle idee davvero chiare. E poi lui ha sempre una pista, può sempre rendere una canzone più bella coi suoi suoni. E' davvero un grande organista d'accompagnamento. Non é che abbia un vero retroterra di accordi o cose del genere, ma ha una buona testa per le linee.

E questo é Pigpen.

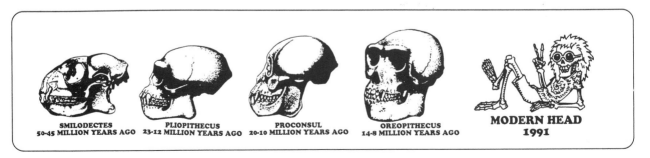

SMILODECTES
50-45 MILLION YEARS AGO

PLIOPITHECUS
23-12 MILLION YEARS AGO

PROCONSUL
20-10 MILLION YEARS AGO

OREOPITHECUS
14-8 MILLION YEARS AGO

MODERN HEAD
1991

And Bill, the drummer's interest has been like jazz drumming and he also played with a lot of big James Brown-style bands, that kind of rhytm and blues, very fast.
And a lot of heavy drum kicks and that show-band kind of stuff.
And he was always the fastest, most heaviest rock'n'roll drummer in Palo Alto, in that whole scene.
And he worked in the same music store that I did. I was teaching guitar and he was teaching drums and we got together quite a bit.
Bob Weir, who plays rhytm, did the whole folk-blues coffeehouse thing.
That was his thing. And he also played jug and kazoo in the jug band when we were playing.
And he's a student, you might say.
His musical leader was Jorma.
He used to go every time Jorma played when he played in coffeehouses Weir'd go there with his tape recorder, tape the whole show and talk to Jorma extensively and watch him play the stuff and study it all and go home and work it out.
Jorma is where he learned a lot of his technique and learned a lot of...
His whole approach to guitar playing was like Jorma's essentially.
Except he's not as good as Jorma, of course.
But his background is that way and in that way and in that folk sort of light blues and a lot of full-voiced chords and finger style.
That's the big thing he's been into.
Like we've all been playing electric instruments for as long as the band's been together, so we're all novices. Like there's guys around that have been playing for ten years, nothing but electric music, like Mike Bloomfield and them have been doing that. We're all new at it.
So that like we hung together and we didn't steal too many ideas from records, try to do too many other people's material.
Instead we'd listen to anything that was good and pick ideas from that andwork at it that way.

E Bill, gli interessi del batterista sono stati nel jazz, ha anche suonato con molte big bands tipo James Brown, quel genere di rhytm and blues, molto veloce. Stacchi di batteria e quel tipo di orchestre spettacolo.
E lui era sempre il più veloce, il più pesante batterista rock'n'roll di Palo Alto, di tutta la scena.
E lavorava nello stesso negozio di musica dove lavoravo io. Io insegnavo chitarra e lui nsegnava batteria e così ci mettemmo insieme per un pò.
Bob Weir, che suona la ritmica, ha fatto tutto il giro delle coffee-houses.
Questo era il suo genere.
Suonava anche jug ed il kazoo nelle jug bands quando noi ci suonavamo.
E poi é uno studente, come sai. Il suo maestro musicale era Jorma.
Non mancava mai quando Jorma suonava.
Era buffo vederlo lì col suo registratore, incideva tutto il concerto e parlava a lungo con Jorma, lo vedeva suonare, studiava il tutto e andava a casa a lavorarci sopra.
E' da Jorma che ha imparato molto della sua tecnica e molto... il suo intero approccio alla chitarra è essenzialmente come Jorma.
Ad eccezione del fatto che non é bravo come Jorma, naturalmente. Ma lui viene da queste cose, da questa sorta di folk blues leggero e di accordi a piena voce e dall'arpeggio.
Questi i suoi grandi amori.
E siccome abbiamo cominciato a suonare strumenti elettrici da quando abbiamo messo insieme la band, possiamo considerarci tutti dei novellini.
Anche se qui c'é in giro gente che ha suonato per dieci anni nient'altro che roba elettrica, tipo Mike Bloomfield, loro hanno fatto queste cose.
Noi siamo nuovi nel genere.
E' come se, girando in giro, avessimo cercato di non rubare troppe idee dai dischi, cercando di eseguire molto materiale altrui.
Abbiamo invece ascoltato tutto quel che ci sembrava buono, prendendo delle idee e lavorandoci sopra.

It's an interesting thing to me that the sound that the band makes is instantly identifiable.

I know. There's a very typical sound.

Yeah, it's obviously The Grateful Dead, it doesn't sound like anybody else.

I know; I can't describe that, I can only say that that's because after working at it and playing together and that's the thing we like to do, that's the result of it. I don't know anything else more about it except that's what it sounds like now.

Trovo interessante che il suono della band sia subito identificabile.

Capisco. E' un suono molto tipico.

Sì, è ovvio che sono i Grateful Dead, non suona come nessun altro.

Capisco, non lo posso descrivere, posso solo dire che ci abbiamo lavorato suonando assieme e che questo é quel che ci va di fare, questo è il risultato. Non so che altro dire, eccetto che adesso suoniamo così.

Free concert - Haigh Street, 1967

What are you trying to do?

Get better! Get better! I mean, like I think of myself as being a student guitarist. I'm try to learn how to play. That's the way I feel about it. I'm trying to learn more about music, more about my playing music. And what... the direction we're trying to go in as of now, after the record, the first record is completed, it kind of put us in a diferent place. What we're trying to do now is expand ourselves musically and that means to get into other things that haven't yet been introduced into popular music and we're... we've been working with musical... it's difficult to explain.
Our approach so far to all our music has been more or less intuitive. And all the arrangements that are on the record are arrangements that we've arrived at through playing the songs.
That's the natural way they go, the sum of us.
We have never written out charts or made leadsheets or arranged parts for specific instruments, we've instead just, like, played it.
And they've settled into arrangements.
Now we're working on arrangements but we're trying also to not arrange our material to death, do you know what I mean?
So we're like we're someplace where we don't know that anybody else is in the same place, so we don't know what to, there's no one guiding us at this point and we're just left to our own devices.
We realize that the one thing that we have to do is to continue to grow as musicians and to continue to expand our outlook on music, to listen to more music and to just get into it.
Keep getting into it heavier and heavier so we can continue to do new things.
And that's what we're trying to do is continue to do new things, I guess.

One of the things that has interested me in listening to the groups in the last year is the whole role of the drums in the electric bands. The drummer seems to me to be a captive.

Cosa state cercando di fare?

Di fare meglio! Di fare meglio! Voglio dire, mi sembra di essere uno che studia la chitarra. Sto cercando di imparare come suonare. Così mi sento. Sto cercando di imparare di più della musica, di più sul mio suonare la musica. A che altro... la direzione in cui cerchiamo di andare adesso, dopo il disco, il primo disco é completato, penso ci porti in luoghi diversi. Quel che stiamo cercando di fare ora é espanderci musicalmente, il che vuol dire occuparsi di altre cose che ancora non sono entrate nella musica popolare e siamo... abbiamo lavorato con musicalità... é difficile da spiegare. Il nostro approccio alla lunga a tutta la nostra musica é stato più o meno intuitivo. E tutti gli arrangiamenti che sono sul disco sono arrangiamenti cui siamo arrivati suonando i pezzi. Questa é la via naturale che prendono, la somma di tutti noi. Non abbiamo mai scritto spartiti o arrangiato delle parti per strumenti specifici, ma li abbiamo semplicemente suonati. E tutto ciò ha dato vita agli arrangiamenti. Tuttora stiamo lavorando a degli arrangiamenti ma stiamo anche cercando di non arrangiare il nostro materiale all'infinito, capisci quel che voglio dire? E' come se ci trovassimo nello stesso posto senza che nessuno sappia di esserci, e non sappiamo com'é, non c'é nessuno che ci guida a questo punto ed ognuno si arrangia per sè.
Abbiamo capito che quel che dobbiamo fare é continuare a crescere come musicisti e continuare ad allargare il nostro sguardo sulla musica, ascoltare più musica per capirla meglio.
Cercare di entrarci sempre di più in modo da continuare a fare nuove cose. Ed é quel che stiamo cercando di fare: continuare a fare nuove cose, o almeno lo spero.

Una delle cose che hanno destato il mio interesse nell'ascolto dei gruppi l'anno scorso è il ruolo ricoperto dal batterista nelle formazioni elettriche. A volte mi sembra quasi un prigioniero.

I'll tell you. I would realy like for you to be in a situation where you can hear Bill play.

The way he plays... what we're thinking about is, we're thinking, we're trying to think away from solo lines. From the standard routine of these members' comp, this member leads. We're trying to think of ensemble stuff, you know.

Not like dixieland ensemble stuff, something else which we don't yet know anything about.

The way Bill plays is he plays a little with everybody. So like if I'm playing a line, he knows enough about my playing and my thinking, since we've been playing together for all this time, that he can usually anticipate the way I'll think a line.

And he's a great rhytmic reinforcement for any line that I can play, no matter how it relates to the rest of the time going on.

He also plays beautifully with Phil, the bass player. In a standard rock'n'roll band, the way they work is the bass and drums generally work together as a unit. Like Motown records are the clearest example of that.

And that's one way of describing the rhytmic situation.

What we're trying to do is get out of that into where the rhytm is more implied and less obvious. Where it's there all the time and it's there heavy enough so that you can dance to it, but not everybody is playing on the two and four.

So that something else is happening.

And Phil's way of approaching the bass is so utterly different than any other bass players', 'cause he doesn't listen to any bass players.

He listens to his mind! And so the kind of lines he comes put with are so fantastic. He's an amazing bass player. He plays with Bill a lot, and because of the way Phil plays, he makes it impossible for Bill to rely on an old pattern, on a standard-type pattern.

The problem we're having with all this is because all of us still think so musically straight, really, that it's difficult to get away from that and it's difficult to get used to not hearing the heavy two and four.

Ti dirò. Vorrei proprio che tu fossi in una situazione dove poter sentire Bill che suona. Il modo in cui suona... quel che pensiamo, quel che cerchiamo di pensare e di lasciar perdere i discorsi solisti. Chi dovesse avere questi spazi si troverebbe in una posizione guida. Noi cerchiamo di pensare in termini di complesso, capisci. Non un insieme tipo dixieland, ma qualcosa d'altro che ancora non conosciamo bene. La maniera in cui Bill suona è suonare un pò con tutti.

E così se io sto tenendo una linea, lui ne sa abbastanza in merito al mio suono e a quel che sto pensando, dato che abbiamo suonato assieme per tutto questo tempo, tanto che solitamente capisce in anticipo il modo in cui svilupperò una tale linea. E poi é un grosso rinforzo ritmico per qualsiasi cosa io possa suonare, senza problemi rispetto al tempo in cui ci si trova. Suona molto bene anche con Phil, il bassista. Nella classica rock'n'roll band il lavoro di basso e batteria viene generalmente inteso come un tutt'uno... I dischi Motown ne sono un chiaro esempio. E questa è una maniera di descrivere la situazione ritmica. Quel che noi stiamo cercando di fare é uscire da questa forma per un ritmo che sia più implicito e meno ovvio.

Dove sussista per tutto il tempo e ci stia in maniera abbastanza sostenuta da poterlo ballare, senza per questo che tutti suonino in quattro quarti. Dunque qualcosa sta succedendo.

E poi l'approccio di Phil al basso é talmente diverso rispetto a qualsiasi altro bassista, perché lui non sta mai ad ascoltare altri bassisti. Lui ascolta la sua testa! E così le linee che vengono fuori sono fantastiche. E' un bassista straordinario. Suona tanto con Bill e proprio per come suona Bill diventa per quest'ultimo impossibile fermarsi su un vecchio motivo o su qualcosa di codificato. I problemi che abbiamo con tutto ciò vengono dall'essere tutti così musicalmente quadrati, davvero, ed é difficile allontanarsi da questo stato, com'é difficile abituarsi a non sentire il quattro quarti.

It's difficult to think rhytmically without having it there all the time but we're starting to develop that sense better. The time thing is the whole big problem, as far as I know.

When you're on the stage playing, what instrument do you hear the loudest?

Mine. Because I'm standing right in front of it.

Do you hear the drums?

I always put myself right next to the drums.
I always listen to the drums and I always listen to Phil. And if I move out in front, I can hear Bob. Sometimes we work it so that dynamics drop, so that the bass and organ drop a little so that me and Bob work together.
We try it so that we all work together one way or another, any way that it happens.
What we're trying to do is free all ourselves from any of us having to 'comp, any of us having to play flat rhytm.
Do you know what I mean?

E' difficile pensare in termini di ritmo senza averlo lì per tutto il tempo ma stiamo cominciando a sviluppare meglio questo senso. Il fattore tempo è il grosso problema, almeno per me.

Quando sei sul palco a suonare, qual'é lo strumento che senti più forte?

Il mio. Perché ci sono proprio davanti.

Senti la batteria?

Mi metto sempre vicino ai tamburi. Ascolto sempre la batteria e ho sempre nelle orecchie Phil. E se mi muovo in avanti, posso sentire Bob. Spesso facciamo in modo che le dinamiche siano un pò più basse, cosicché basso ed organo calino un pò in modo che io e Bob si riesca a lavorare insieme. Noi ci proviamo, in modo da poter lavorare insieme in una maniera o nell'altra, in qualsiasi modo vada. Quel che cerchiamo di fare é liberare tutti noi da uno stretto legame con gli altri, ognuno di noi suona su un semplice ritmo, capisci quel che voglio dire?

710 Haigh Street

Will you hang that on the rhytm guitar then?

No, because Bob doesn't play flat rhytm. He doesn't play hardly any of that kind of rhytm at all. He plays a whole other thing.
He plays these other kinds of lines and stuff like... he works out this very lovely kind of stuff most of the time. There's not that feeling of the big rhytm going, because we do a lot of tricks within a bar and the trick that we do is like eliminating the beat entirely and just all of us not playing it.
Like we're starting to use the space rather than the time or whatever...

You imply it.

That's what we're trying to do. And yet keep it groovy and yet make it so that people can still move to it. 'Cause that's, I think that we still feel that our function is as a dance band.
We feel that our greatest value is as a dance band and that's what we like to do.
We like to play with dancers. We like to see it and really, nothing improves your time like having somebody dance.
Just like pulls the whole thing together. And it's also a nice little feedback thing.

E poi ti leghi alla chitarra ritmica?

No, perché Bob non suona ritmi piani. Lui non suona nessun genere di ritmo del tutto. Suona tutta un'altra cosa. Suona questi altri tipi di linee e roba tipo... tira fuori queste belle cose tutte le volte. Non c'è questo sentimento del grande ritmo, perché abbiamo un sacco di trovate dentro ogni accordo e gli accorgimenti che usiamo portano ad eliminare quasi completamente la battuta e tutti noi non la suoniamo. Come se cominciassimo ad usare lo spazio piuttosto che il tempo o chissà che altro...

Lo dai per scontato.

Questo é quel che cerchiamo di fare. E di andare avanti in questo senso in modo da far muovere la gente. Perché é così, penso che noi si abbia ancora la funzione di un gruppo che faccia ballare. Pensiamo che il nostro valore più grosso stia nell'essere un gruppo che fa ballare ed é questo che ci piace fare. Ci piace suonare con dei ballerini. Ci piace vederli e davvero, nulla da più vigore al tuo tempo che avere qualcuno che ci balla. Proprio come se fosse una cosa sola. Ed é anche una cosa carina avere una risposta del genere.

And I've heard the people stomping on the floor, I hadn't heard that since the Count Basie bands when they'd take a break and everybody's time was just going right on along.
Everybody's in the band!

Right. That's the ideal situation.
Everybody should be in the band! And when that's happening, it's really something special. It's an amazing thing.

People get very hung up about the volume.

That's true. Because it's very loud! But there's something to that too. There's something to that, too. And the thing that I've found is when I'm at one of the dance halls and a band's playing, it's foolish for me to try to tell anybody anything, or say anything to anybody because they can't hear me. The band's roaring away.
And I would just as soon have that. And it's like being in a place where there're no lights. You are less self-conscious if you can't be heard, so you don't mind screaming. And if nobody can see you, you can dance any way you want! It's like that kind of thing, you know. It's just... I think of it as being a sensory overload, or something like that. I don't think it's a bad thing.

I did in the beginning but I don't anymore; I got used to it.

Drives the old folks crazy. Too loud!

Well, there's different ways of being loud.

Right.
That's another thing that we're getting into.
Like the big thing that we see is how loud everything is.
Because taht's the big problem we deal with continually.
The thing we're working on is dynamics.

Ho anche sentito gente battere il piede, non lo sentivo dai tempi delle orchestre di Count Basie quando prendevano lo stacco per riprendere ogni volta il tempo.
Ognuno fa parte del gruppo!

Giusto. Questa é la situazione ideale. Ognuno dev'essere della banda! E quando questo accade, é davvero una cosa speciale. E' una cosa straordinaria.

La gente é molto colpita dal volume.

E' vero. Perché é tanto alto! Ma c'é da dire qualcosa in proposito. C'é un motivo. Quello che ho trovato io é che quando mi trovo in una sala da ballo e un gruppo sta suonando, é pazzesco per me cercare di dire qualcosa a qualcuno, per il semplice fatto che non mi può sentire. La band fa sentire il suo suono di brutto. E mi piacerebbe raggiungere presto questo stato. E' come trovarsi in un posto quando non ci sono luci. Hai meno consapevolezza di te se non puoi essere ascoltato, e così non tenti neanche di urlare. E se nessuno può vederti tu puoi ballare come ti pare! E' una cosa così, capisci... Vedo la cosa come un sovraccarico sensoriale, o qualcosa del genere. Non mi sembra una cattiva cosa.

Mi é capitato agli inizi, ma ora non più, mi ci sono abituato.

Fa impazzire quelli più in là negli anni. Troppo alto!

Beh, ci sono molti modi per essere alto.

Vero.
Questa è un'altra faccenda di cui ci stiamo interessando.
La cosa grossa che vorremmo vedere é quanto alta ogni cosa possa essere sparata. Perché é questo il grosso problema con cui abbiamo a che fare di continuo. Stiamo lavorando sulle dinamiche.

With electric instruments, dynamics are a little bit tricky. Because it necessitates either turning down your volume or really developing a good touch on an electric instrument. And now we've got... the way our stuff is working now it's starting to develop natural dynamics of its own. This is a new thing, just new. That's why we want to work in the clubs and work in these places so we can develop that. The more we play, the better it gets. In a club we've gotten... like we've spent two years with loud and we've spent six months with deafening! I think that we're moving out of our loud stage.

The whole thing about loud is this, is that when you're in a huge place... The thing we're thinking about, what happened was, we went to the very first Family Dog show stoned on acid, or maybe it was the second one, the one where the Lovin' Spoonful were. And we came in there.

We just had our bang going, we'd been playing out in these clubs and stuff and we went in there and we heard the thing. And from the back of the hall you couldn't hear anything. You could hear maybe the harmonica.

As you moved around you could hear a little of something, a little of something else but you could never hear the whole band, unless you were right in front of it and in that case you couldn't hear the vocal. So in our expanding consciousness, we thought, the thing to do, obviously, when you play in a big hall, is to make it so that you can hear everything everywhere.

How do we go about this, we thought?

And the most obvious thing was, we just turn up real loud! But that's not sxactly where it is.

We've learned that what's really important is that the music be groovy.

And if it's groovy enough and if it's well played enough, it doesn't have to be too loud, if it has the definition.

It's more important that it be clear than loud. It would be nice if it were both loud and clear.

That's something you can't do with electric instruments.

Con una strumentazione elettrica le dinamiche possono giocare qualche scherzo dato che a volte necessitano un abbassamento di volume per ottenere un buon tocco sullo strumento elettrico. Ed ora noi abbiamo preso... la maniera in cui le nostre cose funzionano é verso uno sviluppo delle dinamiche naturali. E' una cosa nuova, proprio una novità. Ecco perché vogliamo lavorare nei clubs ed in questi posti dove si possa sviluppare questa cosa. Più suoniamo e meglio vanno le cose. In un club abbiamo preso... come se avessimo passato due anni con l'alto volume e sei mesi con l'assordamento! Penso che stiamo uscendo dalla nostra fase rumorosa.

Il fatto é che tutto questo rumore, quando ti trovi in un posto grosso... Se pensiamo a quel che é successo nel nostro primo concerto per la Family Dog quando eravamo tutti in acido, o forse era il secondo, quello dove c'erano i Lovin' Spoonful. E c'eravamo anche noi. Avevamo appena iniziato con la band, suonavamo in questi clubs, arrivavamo lì e sentivamo quel che c'era. E dal fondo della sala non riuscivi a sentire niente. Riuscivi forse a sentire l'armonica. Se ti muovevi un pò potevi sentire un pò di qualcosa o un pò di qualcos'altro ma non riuscivi mai a sentire l'intera band, a meno di starci proprio di fronte e, in tal caso, non potevi sentire il cantante. Così, con l'ampliarsi delle nostre conoscenze abbiamo pensato che la cosa da farsi, ovviamente, quando si suona in una grossa sala, é di fare il possibile affinché si senta bene da tutte le parti. Come arrivare a questo, ci siamo detti? E la cosa più ovvia era di dare al massimo il volume! Ma questo non é esattamente quel che ci vuole. Abbiamo imparato che quel che importa davvero é che la musica sia piacevole. E se é abbastanza piacevole ed é suonata abbastanza bene non é il caso di spararla tanto forte, una volta raggiunta la definizione.

E più importante la chiarezza che l'altezza del volume. Sarebbe bello avere tutt'e due le cose: chiaro e forte. Ma é qualcosa che non puoi fare con gli strumenti elettrici.

The volume is a device a lot. And it's a good device if you are able to use it well and it's even musical if you are able to use it well, but it's a problem. It's a problem because of the lack of definition involved. And then there's actual technical problems when you're playing on a stage. Certain frequencies of your instrument are washed out by the same frequencies in other instruments. Other electrical instruments. So that in order to hear yourself play you have to be a little bit louder. And you can see what happens. Everybody starts to turn up a little bit so by the end of the night everybody's creeped up so they're real loud. And these kind of things happen.

There's all kinds of freak stuff that happens electronically. Sound against sound. When you have two notes that are aproximately in tune but not quite in tune, this whole other thing starts to happen and that's something else we're getting into. The subharmonic or the harmonic over the... Whenever you play an interval of two notes on two different strings on a guitar you also get the sum of the two notes, either an octave below or an octave above. And depending on how good your equipment is, that's how good you'll be able to hear it. There are lots and lots of books on vibrating-string principles and lots of amazing stuff happens. You can play... I've taken to playing some runs that are in open fifths, parallel fifths. Just the whole run is played that way and that gives me the run an octave below the fundament. The same run. And maybe nobody notices it, but I notice it! And those phenomena are things that really start to get interesting. Like when you get feedback from a fretted note. And the feedback is a strong sustained tone, if you slowly move the string, stretch the string, so that it raises in about quarter-steps or eight-steps, you can also raise the feedback in quarter-steps and eight-steps. So that you can slur all the way up to a note, have the sustained note you shouldn't be able to get on a guitar. It's a whole other principle using the sustained...

Il volume é un congegno. Ed è un buon aggeggio se riesci ad usarlo bene ed é anche musicale se lo sai adoperare come si deve, ma rimane un problema. E' un problema per la perdita di definizione che implica. E poi ci sono problemi tecnici quando suoni su un palco. Certe frequenze del tuo strumento sono spazzate via dalle stesse frequenze in altri strumenti. Altri strumenti elettrici. E così se vuoi sentirti suonare devi dare un pochino su il volume. E allora puoi capire cosa sta succedendo. Ognuno dà su un poco così alla fine della serata facendo finta di niente si arriva ad un volume davvero alto. E queste sono le cose che succedono. C'é tutta questa roba da matti che può capitare con l'elettronica. Suono contro suono. Quando ti trovi due note che sono approssivamente in sintonia ma non abbastanza sintonizzate, viene fuori tutta un'altra cosa e ti trovi in qualcosa del tutto differente. Le subarmoniche o le armoniche sopra le... Ogni volta che suoni un intervallo di due note su due corde diverse della chitarra hai anche la somma delle due note, anche un ottava sotto o un ottava sopra. E, in base alla validità dell'impianto, sarai capace di sentirla. Ci sono un sacco di libri sui principi di vibrazione delle corde ed un sacco di cose straordinarie possono succedere. Puoi suonare... Ho cominciato a suonare alcuni giri in quinte aperte, quinte parallele. L'intero giro é suonato in questa maniera, in modo da darmi il giro di un ottava sotto quello di base. Lo stesso giro. E può anche darsi che nessuno se ne accorga, ma io sì che me ne rendo conto! E questi fenomeni sono cose che cominciano a diventare davvero interessanti.

Come il feedback che ti ritrovi quando fai una nota su un certo tasto.

E il feedback va ancora più su; se tocchi dolcemente la corda o la tiri, di un quarto o di un'ottava, anche il feedback sale di questi valori.

Allora il tutto si impasta in una nota, una nota dominante che non riusciresti a tirar fuori da una chitarra.

E' tutta un'altra faccenda se usi il sustain...

This is a whole other instrument you're playing anyway.

Really. Really it is. It's like when I pick up a regular flat-top plain old traditional guitar, I can hardly play it. You know my touch is developed for the light responsiveness I like in an electric guitar. And I'm used to the way an electric guitar feels and the way they respond, it's a whole other thing. And even playing the electric guitar without the electricity is not playing an electric guitar. And there's also different responses that you get at different volumes, that's another thing. So like if I want my guitar to have a certain characteristic sound, it won't get it any way except for me to turn up my amplifier to a certain point. Then I know that sound, it'll produce that particular sound. That's part of the stuff that we're dealing with, is the actuality of what happens between the guitar, the amplifier and the speakers. So the stuff that comes out is not always what you expect.

It depends a lot on how you have it set; rather than fool with the knobs on my guitar, which I do a lot more for dynamic change than anything else, at a certain volume the tone changes are coming from the amplifier and then it's a matter of my going to the amplifier and turning it up a little or turning it down a little or changing one of the tonal responses a little so that it develops another thing.

There's a whole series of feedback cycles where if you play a note and get feedback on it, you get that note an octave lower plus its fifth. Sometimes it pops an octave higher and then another octave higher yet.

Can you predict it?

I'm getting so I can. I can't predict it to the point because it depends a lot like on how old the strings are, you know, and how close I am to the amplifier. And if I'm in a certain field by the amplifier, I can get certain kinds of pickup. Certain kinds of feedback.

Allora è tutto un altro strumento quello che ti trovi a suonare.

Davvero. E' proprio così. Come quando suono una vecchia chitarra di tipo tradizionale, faccio fatica a suonarla. Capisci che il mio tocco si é sviluppato in base alla chiara risposta che si ottiene da una chitarra elettrica. Ed io sono abituato a sentire una chitarra eletrica ed il tipo di risposta che mi dà, è tutta un'altra cosa. Ed anche suonando la chitarra elettrica senza elettricità non é come suonare una chitarra elettrica. E ci sono differenti risposte anche se cambia il volume, e questo é un altro aspetto ancora. Così, se voglio ottenere dalla mia chitarra un certo suono caratteristico, non avrò altro modo di raggiungerlo se non portando l'amplificatore a determinati livelli. Questo suono io lo conosco, é così che si producono suoni particolari. E' giusto quanto stiamo facendo, l'attualità di quel che succede tra la chitarra, l'amplificatore e le casse.

Quel che ne esce non é sempre quel che ti aspetti. Dipende molto da come hai preparato le cose; piuttosto che impazzire con le manopole della mia chitarra, cosa che faccio più di chiunque altro per i cambi di dinamica, ad un certo volume i cambi di tono vengono dall'amplificatore ed é per questo che lo devo regolare su o giù o cambiare una delle risposte di tono quanto basti per sviluppare altre sonorità. C'é un'intera gamma di cicli di feedback entro cui suonare una nota con un certo ritorno, avrai una nota più bassa di un'ottava più la sua quinta. A volte va su di un'ottava e di un'altra ancora.

Tu lo puoi sapere?

Cerco di farlo. Ma non posso sapere fino in fondo quel che ne verrà fuori perché questo dipende molto dallo stato delle corde, capisci, e di quanto sono vicino all'amplificatore.

E se mi trovo in un determinato campo rispetto all'amplificatore posso raggiungere certi effetti.

It's very tricky stuff 'cause there's so many elements involved in it.

It's a kind of electronic music.

Yeah, it really is. It's electronic music in its practical application. The music itself, that's the thing about the studio, see, is that this stuff doesn't happen that much in the studio beause you aren't playing the kind of volumes where that kind of stuff wil happen, although on the record I was loud enough to get some of that, that feedback pops in here and there. It's a matter now that we have this new thing, these electronic sounds, it's a question of how can you use them in such a way so that they are musical rather than just racket? Because the point is fine. I've been using the feedback stuff instead of for playing lines or for producing a layer of sound which is the thing that happens most naturally. I've been using it by like striking a string and bringing up my volume knob so that there is no attack on the beginning of the note. The note just starts to come out of the air. 'Cause I've already played the string, turn up the volume, the feedback starts. And I stop the string at a rhytmical interval. So that I have... if I were to draw a picture of the tone, it would be just about the reverse of what a guitar tone normally is where you have a heavy attack and then a slow decay. Because it's the other way around, it decays in and attacks off. So I use it as a rhythmic device more than anything else. In that particular thing. But you know, the more it happens, the more I know about it and the more ideas I get for it and so forth. It's just a matter of playing more.

How much do you play a day?

We put in about six, seven hours a day.
Down at the studio, like going over material, working on new ideas or something like that or just goofing off.
And if we're working a gig, then it's the gig.

Certo feedback, ci sono molti accorgimenti visti i vari elementi che concorrono al risultato finale.

E' una specie di musica elettronica.

Sì, é davvero così. E' musica elettronica nella sua applicazione pratica. La musica stessa, e qui ritorniamo allo studio di registrazione, vedi, non é proprio così quando sei in sala d'incisione, proprio perché non suoni a quel volume che ti serve per dare certi suoni, anche se pure su disco siamo abbastanza alti da arrivarci vicino, il feedback salta fuori qui e là. E' un dato di fatto che abbiamo a che fare con questi nuovi aspetti, questi suoni elettronici, la questione é come utilizzarli in modo che siano musicali e non fracassoni. E' un punto delicato. Ho usato il feedback invece di suonare linee normali per cercare suoni il più naturali possibile. L'ho usato maltrattando una corda e dando su la manetta del volume in modo che non vi sia un attacco all'inizio della nota. La nota comincia proprio come se uscisse dall'aria. Perché io ho già suonato sulla corda e aumentato il volume, ed il feedback dà i suoi effetti. E mollo la corda ad intervalli ritmici. Ottengo così... Se dovessi fare un disegno della tonalità, sarebbe quasi il contrario di quel che é normalmente la tonalità di una chitarra, quando ti trovi ad avere un attacco pesante e poi un lento abbassamento. Perché qui é proprio il contrario, entro dolcemente e ne esco con potenza. Uso questo sistema in senso ritmico più di qualsiasi altra cosa. In questi effetti particolari. Ma, capisci, più lo faccio, più ne capisco e più idee mi vengono fuori. E' solo una faccenda di suonare sempre di più.

Quanto suoni in un giorno?

Ci lavoriamo sei, sette ore al giorno. Allo studio, prendiamo del materiale e lavoriamo sulle nuove idee o ce la passiamo.
Se invece si tratta di preparare un concerto, allora facciamo il concerto.

Actually, the best practice there is is playing the gig.

How much of your material is completely original?

I'd say about 40 percent of it. And it's only completely original in that it's our choice of elements. The elements, in terms of their relationships from one to another, are still essentially the same. The relationships are standard kinds of relationships. They aren't too weird. Although we have a few songs that have like tritone relationships and we've even got one now, this is the kind of things we're trying to work into, we have this song called *New potato caboose* and it's not on the record or anything, it'll probably be on the next album, it's a very long thing and it doesn't have a form, in that it doesn't have a verse-chorus form. We took it from a friend of ours who's a poet named Bobby Petersen who wrote us this thing. And we just set it and it instead is a whole thing. It has two or three recurring elements, but it doesn't have a recurring pattern, it just changes continually, off of itself and through itself in lots of different ways. Rhytmically and the tonality of it and the chord relationships. There's a lot of surprises in it, a lot of fast, difficult kind of transitions. And there are transitions that musicaly are real awkward. They're not the kind of thing that flows at all but we're trying to make this happen by trying something that's just jarring and making it not jarring. Making it so that it happens without anybody losing their mind when it happens! And just to see if we can do it. And the thing, as it is, is a little stilted because we aren't yet, we aren't really able to get with it.
'Cause it's all so utterly, so odd. But it has its points and I think that's like one direction that we'll be able to move successfully in.

What kind of music do you listen to, other than going to places around?

Everything. Anything.

Davvero, la pratica migliore in questi casi è fare un concerto vero e proprio.

Quanto del vostro materiale è del tutto originale?

Direi il 40 per cento. Quello che c'é di completamente originale é la nostra scelta di elementi. Gli elementi, in termini di legatura l'uno con l'altro, sono sempre essenziali. Le legature sono già più definite. Non sono così particolari. Anche se abbiamo qualche pezzo con legature tritonali ed anche adesso ne stiamo facendo una, questo é il genere di cose su cui stiamo lavorando, abbiamo questa canzone che si chiama *New potato caboose* che ancora non é stata registrata e che probabilmente sarà sul prossimo album, é molto lunga e non ha una forma, non ha una struttura tipo verso-ritornello. L'abbiamo presa da un nostro amico, un poeta di nome Bobby Petersen che ce l'ha scritta. Ci abbiamo lavorato e ne abbiamo fatto una cosa compatta. Ha due o tre elementi ricorrenti ma non un motivo fisso, cambia continuamente, fuori e dentro di sé in molti modi. Per quanto riguarda il ritmo e la tonalità e le legature tra gli accordi. Ci sono un sacco di sorprese, tanti passaggi veloci e difficili. E ci sono passaggi che musicalmente sono davvero terribili. Non é quel genere di cose che viene fuori così, bisogna sbattersi per tirar fuori un'intonazione dalla stonatura. E farlo senza diventarci matti più di tanto! Giusto per vedere se possiamo farcela.
E' una faccenda un attimino artificiosa perché noi ancora non siamo arrivati a questo punto, non ne abbiamo ancora la capacità. Perché é tutto così complessivo, così strano.
Ma rappresenta un punto fermo e penso sia una direzione verso cui andare con possibilità di successo.

Che tipo di musica ascolti, oltre quella dei vari posti dove suonate?

Tutto. Ogni cosa.

If it's good I'll listen to it or if it's around I'll listen to it. I listen to anything that turns me on. Or that somebody turns me on to.

What turns you on?

What can I say? Almost anything I listen to. If it's well-played music... I mean if you're a musician, you know when somebody's really playing, and when they're not really playing. If it's well-played music, I like it. If it's anything, country and western music, jazz, I've been listening to a lot of jazz lately. I've been listening to a lot of Django Reinhardt. Mostly for the guitar, you know. But I've learned as much from the violin player in terms of those really lovely, graceful ideas. And that's the kind of stuff I like. Anything that, like, is beautiful. Indian music. All the things that people listen to, I guess, I listen to, whatever it is. Soul music, rhytm and blues, old-time blues, jug-band music.

Se é buona la ascolto, e così per quel che c'é in giro. Sento tutto quello che colpisce. O che qualcuno mi fa sentire.

Che cosa ti colpisce?

Che posso dire? Quasi tutto quel che ascolto, se é musica ben suonata... Voglio dire, se sei un musicista capisci subito se uno sta davvero suonando o no. Se é musica ben suonata, mi piace. Qualsiasi cosa sia, country & western, jazz, ho ascoltato un sacco di jazz ultimamente, un sacco di Django Reinhardt. Più che altro roba di chitarra, mi capisci.
Ma anche molti violinisti in termini di idee veramente piacevoli. Questo é il genere di roba che mi piace. Tutto é bello. Musica Indiana. Tutto quel che la gente ascolta, pure io lo sento, qualunque cosa sia. Soul, rhytm and blues, vecchio blues, jug-band.

Ken Kesey & the Merry Pranksters

This whole business of blues. Do you get any heat on the racial question on this?

No, we haven't. The places we've played... We've played some pretty hard-edge places, to, we played the Job Corps, where it's all spade kids. We played in a spade show, in fact, like a rhytm and blues show. And we were received, I think we were a shock to them, because the music we were playing was heavy blues, certainly heavier than any of the spade guys were doing, they were doing all the lighter stuff. And we've had different kind of things, like different people have said different things to us.
There are certain guys who are like into the whole black nationalist thing about spade music and about jazz and so forth and they say things like, "Oh, why don't these white boys stop trying to play colored music?" And so forth. But I don't feel, like I don't feel that that's my orientation. And the ideas that I've pulled from blues musicians and from listening to blues are from my affection for the blues which is like since I was a kid. And I've been listening to rhytm and blues as long as there's been rhytm and blues around here, you know. That was one of the first kinds of music I was turned on to.

Questa faccenda del blues. Ci trovi anche un aspetto razziale?

No, per noi non é così. I posti dove abbiamo suonato... Abbiamo suonato anche in posti difficili, tipo il Job Corps, dove sono tutti ragazzi neri. Abbiamo suonato in uno spettacolo da neri, in effetti, come uno spettacolo di rhytm and blues. E ci hanno accettati, penso sia stato uno shock per loro, perché la musica che suonavamo era blues duro, di certo più duro di quanto avesse potuto fare un nero, loro facevano tutte quelle cose più leggere. E poi noi abbiamo una varietà di roba, e così gente diversa ha da dire cose diverse su di noi. Ci sono dei tipi che hanno una visione più vicina al concetto di nazione nera in merito alla musica dei neri al jazz e queste cose, e dicono cose tipo "Perché questi ragazzi bianchi non la smettono di suonare la musica di colore?" e cose del genere. Ma per me non é così, non é questo il mio orientamento. E le idee che abbiamo preso dai musicisti blues ed ascoltando il blues derivano dall'affetto che ho per il blues sin da quando ero un ragazzo. E ho sentito il rhytm and blues da quando ha cominciato a girare da queste parti, lo sai. E' stato uno dei primi generi musicali cui mi sia interessato.

How old are you?

Twenty-four.
I mean, I don't feel unnatural - I don't feel uptite about it, somebody might.
But the stuff that we're doing, if you look at it, it's like got those ideas, blues ideas and spade kinds of dance ideas and stuff like that, but realy musically, in as far as moving yourself goes, those are some groovy ideas and they turn us on.
But a lot of other things turn us on as well. Any kind of well-performed stuff. Whatever it is.
Pigpen has his own style, that is perhaps the sum of lots of styles, but it's nonetheless consistently Pigpen.
He doesn't, like, flash from James Brown to Smokey Robinson.
He stays Pigpen.
And that's because his attitude toward the blues is so, it's been so long and slow and it's been a mellowing process, you know.
At the very begining, his big vocal influence was Lightnin' Hopkins.
And that's who he used to listen to and he could, like, if he wants to, he can sing exactly like Lightnin' Hopkins.
And play the guitar like Lightnin' Hopkins and to the point of being completely irregular about the changes and stuff, just like Lightnin' is. But Pigpen has been into that for such a long time that it's no longer an effort, and it's no longer something that he tries to do.
Like when we give him a song to sing, it comes out Pigpen's way. It's not anything else.

That's a beautiful name. Who gave that to him? You did?

Oh, a long time ago. A long time ago. 'Cause back when he was about 14 or 15 he was almost like he is now and he'd be around, kind of slouching around and wearing these old duds.
He's really a classical figure.

Quanti anni hai?

Ventiquattro.
Voglio dire, non mi sembra una cosa fuori dal normale, non mi sento particolarmente in ansia, anche se a qualcuno potrebbe capitare. Ma le cose che facciamo, se le guardi bene, tipo prendere queste idee, idee blues o del tipo musica nera ballabile, in senso strettamente musicale, sono quelle che ci fanno muovere, sono quelle idee che crescono e che ci danno uno stimolo. Ma un mucchio di altre cose ci danno la carica in maniera altrettanto valida. Ogni genere di roba ben eseguita. Qualsiasi cosa sia. Pigpen ha il suo stile particolare, che é forse una somma di tanti stili, ma ciò non toglie che si tratti chiaramente di Pigpen. Non é che diventi improvvisamente James Brown o Smokey Robinson. Rimane Pigpen. Questa è la sua attitudine verso il blues, una cosa lenta e lunga, un processo di maturazione, capisci. All'inizio la sua voce fu molto influenzata da Lightnin' Hopkins.
Era quello che ascoltava di più e, se avesse voluto, avrebbe potuto cantare esattamente come Lightnin' Hopkins. E suonare la chitarra come Lightnin' Hopkins fino ad arrivare ad essere completamente fuori dalle regole per gli stacchi e tutto il resto, proprio come Lightnin'. Ma Pigpen ci è stato a mollo per così tanto tempo che non occorre più che si sforzi, e non è che si debba sbattere per raggiungere questo genere di cose. Quando gli diamo una canzone da cantare, ne viene fuori alla maniera di Pigpen. Niente a che vedere con chiunque altro.

E' un nome davvero bello. Chi gliel'ha dato? Sei stato tu?

Oh, é passato tanto tempo.
Quando aveva 14 o 15 anni era quasi com'é adesso, camminata ciondolante e questi vecchi stracci.
Una figura davvero classica.

It seems to me that there are social implications to this music which haven't really been dealt with. It's not only the volume and the style and so on, but it represents a whole attitude.

I know it does, but I'd be hard put to define that attitude. Like, the guys that were over interviewing us the other day were talking serious. They wanted to know about the scene and what our motivation was and what about drugs and so forth like that. And the music is doing something else. It has to do with all these things, yes, but I think that the more important thing than just the music is the whole attitude. The dance thing, the whole fact that there are lots of people getting together. And for all of us, this is the first time we've ever seen lots of people get together.
'Cause we never grew up in where there were like dances or things like that. It was pretty isolated and you did some other, like smaller, more intimate stuff. And now suddenly there are large groups of people getting together.
And that seems like the more significant point sociologically.

Mi sembra ci siano anche delle implicazioni sociali di cui ancora non abbiamo parlato in merito a questo tipo di musica. Non si tratta solo di volume, ma di un modo di essere più complessivo.

Lo so che é così, ma è difficile cercare di definire certi atteggiamenti. Come quei tipi che ci stavano intervistando l'altro giorno, parlavano seriamente. Volevano sapere della scena e di quali fossero le nostre motivazioni, e qualcosa sulle droghe e cose simili. E la musica sta facendo delle altre cose. Ha a che fare con tutto ciò, certo, ma io penso che la cosa più importante sia che proprio la musica debba essere la faccenda principale. Il ballare, il fatto che ci siano un sacco di persone che si mettono assieme. E per tutti noi, questa é la prima volta che si vedono così tante persone assieme. Perché non ci é mai capitato prima di essere in posti dove si balli o cose del genere. Erano cose sporadiche e si facevano altre cose, roba più piccola, più intima. E adesso eccoti tutti questi gruppi di persone che si mettono assieme. E credo che questo sia il punto più importante a livello sociologico.

Ralph J. Gleason

The bands are at the center of it, really, as I see it.

All I can say is I don't know why.

Take the bands out of it and it all goes to pieces.

That's true.

It's like the Trips Festival. Which was a drag except when the music made it. You can do all these things but it doesn't feel good without the music.

I know, I'm not sure why. I'm not sure why. That's something that I don't think anybody really knows quite for sure why.
I think that it might be like an excuse.
Here is the reason for being in this place, and there is a reason for moving yourself, because there is this going on.
But on the other hand, if we weren't doing this...
See, it's all very strange because we all came from such far-out backgrounds into the rock'n'roll scene together as a band.
And all this more or less spontaneously in a very short space of time. I really don't know; I don't know why or how. But suddenly it was the thing to do. It was the right thing to do.
And I'm not sure why.
I think it might be like Phil was saying the other day. He mentioned that when he had sort of like run out of his musical bag before, his prior bag, Kennedy has just been assassinated. And things were loking pretty down. And then all of a sudden here was the Beatles movie. Which was like the first time there was something funny going on. It was very high and very up, you know. And high and up looked better than down and out, really.
So high and up was the place to go, I guess.
So that like for me, my musical bag had run out as well, there was no, like, people who were really interested in blue-grass music and nobody to play with and so forth and so on.
It was like a bankrupt scene.

Mi sembra che le bands siano in mezzo a tutto ciò.

Tutto quel che posso dirti é che non so il perché.

Togli le bands e tutto cade in pezzi.

Questo é vero.

Come per i Trips Festival, una noia se non fosse per la musica. Puoi fare tutte queste cose, ma non sembrano venire bene se non c'é la musica.

Lo so, ma non sono sicuro del perché. Non lo so proprio. Mi sembra di capire che nessuno sappia davvero il perché di quanto accada. Penso che sarebbe come cercare una scusa. Questa é la ragione per essere in questo posto, e questa é la ragione per cui ci si deve muovere, perché questo é quanto sta succedendo. Ma d'altro canto, se non avessimo fatto così... Vedi, é tutto molto strano dato che tutti, da retroterra così diversi, arriviamo sulla scena rock'n'roll uniti come band. E tutto ciò più o meno spontaneamente in un tempo davvero breve. Davvero non ne conosco le ragioni; non so come o perché.
Ma improvvisamente era questa la cosa da fare. Era la cosa giusta da fare. E non so il perché. Potrebbe essere come diceva Phil l'altro giorno. Quando stava abbandonando le sue preferenze musicali, le sue principali influenze, Kennedy era appena stato assassinato. E sembrava che le cose precipitassero. E all'improvviso ecco arrivare questo film sui Beatles. Come se fosse la prima volta che accadesse qualcosa di divertente.
Era una cosa molto energetica, che tirava su. E tirarsi su appariva meglio che essere depressi ed abbattuti, di certo.
E così energia e tirarsi su era il posto dove andare, direi. E così é stato per me, ho abbandonato i miei amori musicali perché pareva che non vi fosse nessuno interessato al blue-grass, e nessuno con cui suonare e così via.
Sembrava uno scenario da bancarotta.

Musically it was interesting but there was nothing going on that was any kind of gratification because you never got a chance to play or anything; you never got a chance to perform the thing.

And playing the music is a real immediate, satisfying thing.

It's like if it's going good, everybody knows it's going good, everybody in the band and everybody in the audience and there's something going on. It's faster, you know, it's a faster thing. It doesn't have to do with... You don't have to worry about the form or anything. It's like really cleansing somehow.

That's a good phrase for it. When I saw The Byrds at the... that joint on Broadway, they didn't turn me on there. And I didn't get any feeling that a thing was developing. And it didn't hit me until the Spoonful played Mother's. I went right out of my nut in there, completely.

And it was...I don't know what it was, I've been trying. I heard the Byrds maybe under bad circumstances in there, as one of them was sick a couple of nights.

It just didn't make it for me.

And the people on the floor looked L. A. freaky, as opposed to looking...

San Francisco hip.

Yeah. I don't know what the hell it is. That guy came up with them, that was like their male go-go dancer, Vito, wasn't that his name, he was always on the floor.

Right.

It looked wrong.

Right.

And those bands still do it wrong from L. A. I don't know what the hell it.

Musicalmente erano cose interessanti ma non succedeva niente e non vi era alcuna gratificazione dato che non vi erano possibilità di suonare o di fare qualcosa; non si aveva mai modo di mettere in scena le tue cose. E suonare musica è una cosa immediata, che deve dare soddisfazione. Deve andare bene, tutti devono sapere che sta andando bene, chi fa parte della band e il pubblico e c'é qualcosa che sta succedendo. E' una cosa che accade così in fretta, molto velocemente. Non ha niente a che fare con... Non ti devi preoccupare della forma o di che altro. E' in qualche modo una forma di purificazione.

Ecco una buona definizione. Quando ho visto i Byrds al... in quel buco di Broadway, non é che mi abbiano fatto una particolare impressione. E non ho avuto particolari sensazioni man mano che le cose andavano avanti. Ero rimasto indifferente finché non andai a sentire gli Spoonful al Mother's. Davvero lì sono uscito dal mio guscio, completamente. Era come... non so cosa fosse, ci stavo provando. I Byrds li avevo sentiti in una brutta circostanza, uno di loro si era ammalato per un paio di serate. Non facevano per me. E la gente sulla pista era del tipo fuori di testa di Los Angeles, l'opposto di quel che sembrano essere...

I giusti di San Francisco.

Si, non so che cosa diavolo sia. Quel tipo se ne venne con questi, una specie di ballerino da night, Vito - era questo il suo nome? - che era perennemente in pista.

Giusto.

Sembrava sbagliato.

Giusto.

E queste bands sembra che sbaglino ancora da Los Angeles. Non so perché diavolo.

They do and now why do they? Is the question. I mean, what's the difference? What's the difference is what I'm wondering. And why is it that San Francisco is so much groovier of a place? Why has the scene blossomed so fantastically? For one thing, everybody's in it, that has a lot to do with it. A band is only a band in the sense that they're on the stage.

But really the band is just about... at least, in the early dances, it's changed an awful lot, in the early dances, everybody was a part of the band.
Everybody was stomping on the floor.
And waving their arms around.
And that was a good feeling.

You know, there's other things too, though. Those L. A. bands are all like the Mamas and Papas, they're thought of in terms of going into the studio and making a record. And they're not thought of in terms of playing night after night for people to dance to.

Right. Right. Because they don't have any dance things in L. A. The extent of the dancing in Los Angeles is ten feet off the floor in a glass cage.

Lo fanno, e perché lo fanno? Ecco la domanda. Voglio dire, qual'é la differenza? La differenza é quel che mi aspetto. E perché San Francisco ha una scena tanto più attiva? Perché le cose sono fiorite in maniera così fantastica? Per prima cosa, ci sono dentro tutti, e questo conta molto. Una band é solo una band nel senso che questi stanno sul palco. Ma in fondo una band é giusto... in definitiva, coi primi gruppi da ballo, le cose sono davvero cambiate un casino, quando si é cominciato a ballare ognuno si é sentito parte della band. Ognuno poteva sbattersi come voleva, e agitare le braccia come gli pareva. E ci si sentiva davvero bene.

Ma, sai, ci sono poi altre cose.
Queste bands di Los Angeles sono un pò come i Mamas and Papas, la vedono come un andare in studio e fare un disco. Non la vedono in termini di suonare serata dopo serata perché la gente possa ballare.

Giusto. Giusto. Proprio perché non hanno niente da ballare a Los Angeles. I locali di Los Angeles sono tre metri di pista in una gabbia di vetro.

Everybody watches, like the movies. Except you go to be watched as well. Your car is where you live in L. A. The car radio is where it's at in L. A. Because if you don't have an automobile, you're not even alive in Los Angeles. And their scene is real isolated, you know. They don't have a community in L. A. There is no place. There is nothing down there. And that's the truth. We were down there... For the millions of people down there, there is no place where you can go and cool it and just like be there and not have to worry about what you're doing there. Or worry about someone asking you what you're doing there. They roust you down there. It's really heavy. Nothing like... Well, that's the way the rest of the country is. San Francisco's the only place where you can do that.

I never used to like Bob Dylan until he came out with an electric music. And I'm not sure why I like that more.

I sure liked it a lot more. Boy, when *Bringing it all back home* came out. Yeah, lovely. Very fine guitar player. It just all of a sudden had something going for it. And Bob Dylan was getting a little less heavy. He was having a little more fun with him. And that was nice. That was a nice change. And I remember another thing that turned me on a lot was when I saw Bob Dylan on television.

On the Les Crane show. When he went on there and sang those songs, you know, and just rapped insanely. Beautiful mad stuff. And that like turned us all on, we couldn't believe it. Here was this guy, it was almost like being in the South and seeing a spade on television.

Where do you think this thing is all going to?

Out. Out to the provinces, out to the rest of the world, I think. I don't see where else it can go. And I think San Francisco is getting very, very outrageous, especially during the summer. Who knows? Who knows where it's going to go?

I'm hoping that all this represents another alternative for the world.

Tutti stanno a guardare, a meno che tu non ci vada per essere guardato. La tua macchina é dove vivi a Los Angeles. La radio in auto é quel che conta a Los Angeles. Anche perché se non hai un'automobile non puoi nemmeno definirti vivo a Los Angeles. E la loro scena é davvero isolata, capisci. Non c'é una comunità a Los Angeles. Non c'é un posto. Non c'é niente là. E questa é la verità. Ci siamo stati... Per i milioni di persone che vi abitano, non c'é un posto dove andare e startene tranquillo ed esser lì solo per non aver preoccupazioni su quel che stai facendo. O dove ti devi preoccupare che qualcuno ti chieda cosa ci stai facendo lì. Ti possono anche arrestare. E' davvero pesante. Non come... Beh, come in tutto il paese. San Francisco é l'unico posto dove puoi fare queste cose. Non mi era mai piaciuto Bob Dylan finché non se ne venne fuori con la musica elettrica. E ancora non so perché mi piaccia tanto. E di certo mi piaceva ancora di più. Ragazzi, quando uscì *Bringing it all back home*. Yeah, stupendo. Un grande chitarrista. Di colpo era venuta fuori questa cosa. E Bob Dylan stava diventando un pò meno pesante. Cercava di divertirsi un pò di più. E questo mi piaceva. Un simpatico cambio. Mi ricordo un altra cosa che mi diede una scossa: quando vidi Bob Dylan in televisione. Allo show di Les Crane. Venne lì a cantare queste canzoni, le sai, e poi cominciò a tirar fuori cose in maniera pazzesca. Splendide cose pazzesche. Fu una botta a tutti noi, non potevamo crederci. C'era questo tipo, era come essere nel Sud e vedere un nero alla TV.

Dove credi che stia andando tutto ciò?

Fuori. Fuori, verso la provincia, il resto del mondo, credo. Non vedo dove altro possa andare. E penso che San Francisco stia diventando molto, molto scandaloso, specialmente d'estate.
Chi lo sa?
Chi sa dove stiamo andando? Spero che tutto ciò rappresenti un'alternativa per il mondo.

Like, yeah, let's take it easy and have a good time. It would sure be nice, is all I can say. I don't know where it's going to go, it might all be on the streets of Bombay in the next month. It looks good, is all I can say. In terms that it loks like it's going to get out and it looks like everybody that's into it is into it sincerely. And really intends to do right by the scene in terms of continuing to develop and grow, continue to add to it and continue to, you know, spread the word, whatever.

We decided, when we got together with the band, we were all on our very separate trips, we were all doing our gigs of one sort of another. Surviving one way or another. And we decided at one time or another that we would have to make a total commitment so we, like, just put everything down and hung together. We thought we were either going to make it or not. I mean we're going to do a thing or we're not going to do a thing and the only way we're going to find out is, like, devote our whole attention to it. Maybe the thing, whatever it is that's needed to be able to get into that kind of scene of like surrendering your own little trip for some better trip, maybe, you have to care enough about it or be willing to stop caring about what you've already got, maybe. But I think San Francisco bands hang together through inclination.

And, like, we were all friends before we got together as a band.

We'd all been into various kinds of weird shit together before. We just tought... why not? We learned how to behave as a unit. We all like each other. We've done it all through inclination.

It's an important thing and somehow we manage to hang together. Like when we went to Vancouver and things got real weird, real fast, when we were up there. We went through a lot of bad scenes and got screwed around one way or another.

It was really, like, the five of us hung together just because that's who we are, we're a family more than anything else, you know.

Just in our attitudes towards each other. And it works out best that way. It seems to.

Sì, prendila tranquillamente e passatela bene. Sono sicuro che sarebbe bello, è tutto quel che posso dire. Non so dove stia andando, potrebbe essere per le strade di Bombay il mese prossimo. Sembra buona, è tutto quel che posso dire. Nel senso che sembra si stia espandendo e che chi c'é dentro lo é sinceramente. E davvero vuole fare bene alla scena nel senso di un continuo sviluppo e crescita, continuare a metterci cose e ad allargarsi al mondo, capisci, tutto quanto.

Abbiamo deciso, quando ci siamo messi insieme nella band, noi eravamo ognuno per i fatti suoi, nelle proprie storie, ognuno faceva i suoi concerti, in una maniera o nell'altra. Tirare avanti in un modo o nell'altro. Ad un certo punto abbiamo deciso che avremmo avuto un impegno comune, totale, lasciar perdere ogni cosa e mettersi assieme. Si trattava di vedere se potevamo farcela o no. Voglio dire, o fai una cosa o non la fai e l'unica maniera per uscirne é dedicare tutta l'attenzione a quello che intendi fare. Può anche essere che si debbano abbandonare le piccole storie personali per qualcosa di meglio, può darsi che tu ti ci debba impegnare al massimo o che invece ti sembri già troppo quel che fai, può essere. Ma io penso che le bands di San Francisco abbiano in comune questa tendenza. Anche perché eravamo già tutti amici ancor prima di metterci insieme come gruppo. Eravamo stati tutti in un sacco di storie pazzesche. Abbiamo solo pensato... perché no? Abbiamo imparato a muoverci come una cosa sola. Ci piacciono anche gli altri. Quel che abbiamo fatto è stato seguire le nostre inclinazioni. E' un aspetto importante, e in qualche modo ci diamo da fare per stare insieme. Come quando siamo stati a Vancouver e le cose stavano diventando davvero strane, veloci quando stavamo lì. Ci sono capitate un sacco di brutte storie e a volte sembra che sia una perdita di tempo. Era davvero così, tutti e cinque insieme perché siamo così, siamo una famiglia molto più di chiunque altro, capisci. Nel modo in cui ci rapportiamo agli altri. E così le cose funzionano meglio. Sembra che sia così.

What got you interested in music, really interested in music?

It was the music that we heard. And like at the time we didn't realize that it was not very good. Because it was good to our young ears. It was moving music and it talked about us, the way we wanted to hear about us, apparently. And after a while, once you get into music, you start to hear more about it. As you get out into it...
Like getting away from rock'n'roll, when I was away from rock'n'roll it was going through that whole, the whole Frankie Avalon, Fabian phase and all this plastic nonsense. And it didn't have much vitality. I sort of lost interest in it 'cause the vitality, the energy in it had gone into other channels. For me, it was in folk music.

But, Jerry, wasn't that folk-music period in a sense... I mean, there were great flok-music performers, like Pete Seeger and The Weavers are great performers. Wasn't there a way, though, in which that folk-music thing was kind of an attraction for performers to get into because they thought it was what they ought to be doing?

I think so. Now, I got into it because my intellectual self was growing and I didn't feel that rock'n'roll music was going to be my vehicle for communication, or whatever.
When I got into folk music, I never got into it behind the lyrical content.
I never was into the protest songs.
I was always into... What first attracted me was the sound of it and those kind of modal changes and so forth and the sound of Joan Baez's voice and the sound of her guitar and then into the more complex forms and finaly what I really got into was the instrumental parts.
Instrumental traditional music and so forth.
Because somehow or another I heard in that, musically, something that was more satisfying to me at that time than, like, rock'n'roll was.

Da che cosa deriva il vostro interesse nella musica, quello che vi appassiona veramente?

E' stata la musica che sentivamo. Allora non ci sembrava così brutta. Anzi, sembrava ottima per le nostre giovani orecchie. Era musica per muoversi, e parlava di noi, nella maniera in cui volevamo si parlasse di noi, in apparenza. E dopo un pò, una volta che sei dentro la musica, cominci a capirne sempre di più. Come se ti trovassi in... come allontanarsi dal rock'n'roll, voleva dire uscire dalla fase dei Fabian, dei Frankie Avalon e tutte queste nullità plastificate. Tutto ciò non aveva più molta vitalità. Ho cominciato a perdere interesse proprio perché la vitalità, l'energia che c'era in quella musica erano finite in altri canali. Per me, nella musica folk.

Ma, Jerry, non era quello il periodo in cui la folk music...
Voglio dire, c'erano grandi artisti, come Pete Seeger e gli Weavers, grandi anche loro.
Non é che si è trattato di un genere di attrazione per cui gli artisti pensavano che si dovesse per forza fare?

Penso che sia così. Ma, io mi ci sono avvicinato perché la mia crescita intellettuale non mi faceva più vedere il rock'n'roll come veicolo di comunicazione, e cose del genere. Quando mi sono dato alla folk music, non mi sono mai interessato a fondo dell'aspetto testi. Niente a che vedere con le canzoni di protesta. Era sempre una questione di... Quello che prima di tutto mi ha attratto è stato il tipo di suono e questo genere di cambi modali e così fino ad arrivare al suono della voce di Joan Baez e a quello della sua chitarra e poi in forme più complesse e infine quello che mi ha preso di più sono state le parti strumentali. Musica tradizionale strumentale e cose simili.
Perché in un modo o nell'altro vi trovavo, musicalmente, qualcosa che a quei tempi mi dava più soddisfazione, di più del rock'n'roll.

But the more I got into it, the more it became obvious to me that it was kind of closed circle, you know what I mean? Like, there's a traditional thing going on and at this point in time the traditional thing is largely diffused. There isn't really too many bodies of strong traditional music going on. They've all evolved. Now in the twentieth century the strong forms of traditional music, white traditional music and colored traditional music, essentially, in the United States have gotten into... colored traditional music is jazz and soul music and Chicago blues and so on and the white music has gone into country and western and more heavily charged kinds of that stuff. But still, the same elements are there. It's as strong, all these things are strong as their roots were. I started out into folk music by listening to the Kingston Trio and so forth and as soon as I realized that I could play better than any of them, I lost interest in them and went on to something else! But then the problem was, who wants to hire Flatt and Scruggs or who wants to hire John Lee Hooker, you know? I mean nobody out here knew about him, there were one or two places, The Cabale would maybe have somebody good once in a long time and it was like really scarce. I'd go way out of my way to see somebody good if they were around.

And it's just one of those things; finally mi interest got into it so much that it was getting so esoteric there was no way for me to hear the music. Except to go out and spend enormous amount of money and go through these whole big changes to just get to where I could hear it. And this was the music that I was devoting all my energy to. And the chance to, like, get back to the people is really... It's joy! It's sudden freedom! But all that stuff is still very heavy to a head, I used to listen to all the same stuff as well. It's a funny thing the way the interests have jumped around, but I remember during all that time I'd occasionally turn on the radio to a rock'n'rol station, there would be this utter pap, terrible, featureless music. And that was really an insult.

Ma più c'ero dentro, più diventava ovvio per me che si trattava di un circolo chiuso, capisci quel che voglio dire? C'è questa scena tradizionale che si sviluppa e ad un dato momento la diffusione si fa più ampia. E non é che siano poi venuti avanti grossi nuclei di musica tradizionale. Ci siamo evoluti un pò tutti. Adesso che siamo nel ventesimo secolo le forme più forti di musica tradizionale, quella bianca e quella nera, essenzialmente, negli Stati Uniti si sono trasformate in... la musica tradizionale di colore é il jazz, la soul music, il blues di Chicago e queste cose mentre la musica bianca é diventata il country & western e roba sempre più appesantita. Ma, ancora, eccoci di fronte agli stessi elementi. C'é una forza: tutte queste cose sono forti se hanno delle forti radici. Ho cominciato ad avvicinarmi al folk col Kingston Trio e andando avanti ho realizzato che avrei potuto suonare meglio di tutti loro, così non mi interessavano più e mi sono diretto verso altre cose!

Ma il problema di allora era: chi vuole Flatt & Scruggs, o chi vuole John Lee Hooker, capisci? Nessuno li conosceva fuori dai loro posti, c'erano uno o due locali, The Cabale forse ne avrebbe fatto suonare qualcuno, una volta ogni tanto e con scarsi risultati.

Me li sarei andati a vedere se fossero stati in giro. E questo é uno dei motivi, alla fine il mio interessamento in questi generi stava diventando tanto esoterico che in realtà non mi riusciva di sentire mai musica. A meno di spendere un sacco di soldi per andare a sentirli da altre parti. Questa era la musica cui dedicavo tuta la mia energia. E poi il cambiamento, tornare tra la gente é proprio come... E' gioia! E' libertà istantanea! Ma tutta questa roba può essere troppo pesante per una testa, e continuavo ad ascoltare tutto quanto lo stesso. E' divertente come certi interessi siano saltati fuori, mi ricordo che allora accendevo casualmente la radio su una stazione che faceva rock'n'roll, dove c'era questa terribile pacottiglia senza arte ne parte. Era davvero un insulto.

The rhytm and blues station I wouldn't mind listening to but even in that, the rhytm and blues at that time was going through some kind of sticky changes. It was all very dull; it was before Motown had come out; before Phil Spector had been around. And there wasn't anything exciting going on, there were no new ideas. The point seems to be to try and communicate something or to be in a position where there is more going on than somebody on stage. I mean, like, it would be nice if traditional folk music could be taken out of the art form that it's been put into, it's art music now. Joan Baez is an art singer and Judy Collins is and so forth. And it lacks vitality, it lacks the vitality that those people as individuals are loaded with. Like here on the West Coast, the guys that are into rock'n'roll music have mostly come up through like I have... like me and Jorma for example... up through folk music and through blues and so forth and stuff like that, these simpler forms. On the East Coast, the musicians who are in rock'n'roll bands are starting to be some of the young jazz musicians who are getting into it and who are bringing it a different kind of vitality. Musical vitality. But it seems as though the jazz music as a movement has somewhere along the line lost the relationship to the audience. The people can't make it with it unless it's really fantastic. The thing of having Charles Lloyd at the Fillmore Auditorium is really fantastic. And a jazz group can't hardly play at the Fillmore without tearing the place down. When Bola Sete's little trio played there, they just ripped it up. Communication is getting so good, so much music is available on records And it's so easy to hear anything you want to hear that in another 20 years, every musician in the world will be able to play with every other musician in the world with no problem at all. That'd be really great, you know!

Non avrei preferito la stazione rhytm and blues, anche lì le cose stavano cambiando sul mieloso. Era tutta una vera noia; era prima che uscisse la Motown, prima che fosse in giro Phil Spector. E non c'era niente di eccitante in giro, non c'erano nuove idee.
Direi che la questione sia tentare di comunicare qualcosa o di essere in una posizione dove c'é qualcosa di più che il semplice stare sul palco. Voglio dire, sarebbe bello se il folk tradizionale uscisse dallo stato di arte in cui è stato cacciato, è una sorta di musica artistica adesso. Joan Baez è una cantante artistica, ed é così anche Judy Collins, ed altri. E questo vuol dire una perdita di vitalità, si perde la vitalità che questa gente possiede a livello individuale.
Come qui nella West Coast, quelli che sono nel rock'n'roll ci hanno avuto più a che fare di me... di me e Jorma per esempio... hanno fatto il folk e il blues e roba del genere, queste forme più semplici. Nella East Coast, i musicisti delle rock'n'roll bands cominciano ad essere delle speci di giovani musicisti jazz, che portano con sé un tipo diverso di vitalità. Vitalità musicale. Ma a volte percepire il jazz come movimento può voler dire perdere i contatti con il pubblico. La gente non riesce a seguire, a meno che sia davvero fantastico. Il fatto di avere Charles Lloyd al Fillmore Auditorium è davvero fantastico.
Ed è difficile che un gruppo jazz riesca a suonare al Fillmore senza buttar giù l'ambiente. Quando il piccolo trio Bola Sete ha suonato lì è stato un fiasco. La comunicazione sta diventando talmente buona, c'é in giro tanta buona musica anche su disco che ti puoi sentire quel che vuoi per altri venti anni, ogni musicista al mondo sarà capace di suonare con qualsiasi altro musicista nel mondo senza alcun problema. E questo sarebbe davvero grande, sai!

Ralph J. Gleason
"The Jefferson Airplane and the San Francisco Sound"
Ballantine Books, New York 1969

DEADOGRAPHY
RECORDS·VIDEOS·BOOKS
BOOTLEGS

OFFICIAL DISCOGRAPHY

La sigla EEC si riferisce a dischi prodotti nei paesi europei

THE GRATEFUL DEAD - The golden road (to unlimited devotion), Beat it on down the line, Good morning little schoolgirl, Cold rain and snow, Sitting on the top of the world, Cream puff war, Morning dew, New, new Minglewood blues, Viola Lee blues.
(Warner Bros. WS 1689. Release date March 17th, 1967)
ANTHEM OF THE SUN - That's it for the other one: Cryptical envelopment, Quadlibet for tender feet, The faster we go the rounder we get, We leave the castel, New potatoe caboose, Born cross-eyed, Alligator, Caution (Do not stop on tracks).
(Warner Bros. WS 1749. Release date July 18th, 1968)
AOXOMOXOA - St. Stephen, Dupree's diamond blues, Rosemary, Doin' that rag, Mountains of the moon, China cat sunflower, What's become of my baby, Cosmic Charlie.
(Warner Bros. WS 1790. Release date June 20th, 1969)
LIVE DEAD - Dark star, St. Stephen, The eleven, Turn on your lovelight, Death don't have no mercy, Feedback, And we bid you goodnight.
(Warner Bros. 2WS 1830. Release date December 1969. Double live)
WORKINGMAN'S DEAD - Uncle John's band, High time, Dire wolf, New speedway boogie, Cumberland blues, Black Peter, Easy wind, Casey Jones.
(Warner Bros. 1869. Release date May 1970)
AMERICAN BEAUTY - Box of rain, Friend of the devil, Sugar Magnolia, Operator, Candyman, Ripple, Brokedown palace, Till the morning comes, Attics of my life, Truckin'.
(Warner Bros. WS 1893. Release date Nov. 1970)

GRATEFUL DEAD - Bertha, Mama tried, Big railroad blues, Playing in the band, The other one, Me and my uncle, Big boss man, Me and Bobby Mc Gee, Johnny B. Goode, Wharf rat, Not fade away, Goin' down the road feeling bad.
(Warner Bros. 2WS 1935. Release date October 1971. Double live)
EUROPE '72 - Cumberland blues, He's gone, One more saturday night, Jack Straw, You win again, China cat sunflower, I know you rider, Brown-eyed woman, It hurts me too, Ramble on rose, Sugar Magnolia, Mr. Charlie, Tennessee Jed, Truckin', Epilogue, Prelude, Morning dew.
(Warner Bros. 3WX 2668. Release date November 1972. Triple live)
WAKE OF THE FLOOD - Mississippi half-step uptown toodeloo, Let me sing your blues away, Row Jimmy, Stella Blue, Here comes the sunshine, Eyes of the world, Weather report suite: Prelude, Part I, Part II.
(Grateful Dead Records GD 01. Release date October 15th, 1973)
GRATEFUL DEAD FROM THE MARS HOTEL - Scarlet begonias, Ship of fools, Pride of Cucamonga, Loose Lucy, U.S. blues, Unbroken chain, China doll, Money money.
(Grateful Dead Records GD 102. Release date June 27th, 1974)
BLUES FOR ALLAH - Help on the way, Slipknot!, Franklin's tower, King Solomon's marbles, Stranger than dirt or milkin' the turkey, The music never stopped, Crazy fingers, Sage and spirit, Blues for Allah, Sand castels & glass camels, Unusual occurences in the desert.
(Grateful Dead Records UA/GD. United Artists LA494G. Release date September 1st, 1975)
STEAL YOUR FACE - The promised land, Cold rain and snow, Around and around, Stella Blue, Mississippi half-step uptown toodeloo, Ship of fools, Beat it on down the line, Big river, Black-throated wind, U.S. blues, El Paso, Sugaree, It must have been the roses, Casey Jones.
(Grateful Dead Records GD LA620 J2GD 104.

Release date June 26th, 1976. Double live)
TERRAPIN STATION - Estimated prophet, Dancin' in the streets, Passenger, Samson and Delilah, Sunrise, Terrapin Station Part I: Lady with a fan, Terrapin Station, Terrapin, Terrapin transit, At a siding, Terrapin flyer, Refrain.
(Arista AL 7001. Release date July 27th, 1977)
SHAKEDOWN STREET - Good lovin', France, Shakedown Street, Serengetti, Fire on the mountain, I need a miracle, From the heart of me, Stagger Lee, All new Minglewood blues, If I had the world to give.
(Arista AB 4198. Release date July 15th, 1978)
GO TO HEAVEN - Alabama getaway, Althea, Feel like a stranger, Lost sailor, Saint of circumstance, Antwerp's placebo, Easy to love you, Don't ease me in.
(Arista AL 9508. Release date April 28th, 1980)
RECKONING - Dire wolf, The race is on, Oh babe it ain't no lie, It must have been the roses, Dark hollow, China doll, Been all around this world, Monkey and the engineer, Jack-a-Roe, Deep Elem blues, Cassidy, To lay me down, Rosa Lee Mc Fall, On the road again, Bird song, Ripple.
(Arista A2L 8604. Release date April 1st, 1981. Double acoustic live)
DEAD SET - Samson and Delilah, Friend of the devil, New, new Minglewood blues, Deal, Candyman, Little red rooster, Loser, Passenger, Feel like a stranger, Franklin's tower, Rhytm devils, Space, Fire on the mountain, Greatest story ever told, Brokedown palace.
(Arista A2L 8606. Release date August 1981. Double live)
IN THE DARK - Touch of gray, Hell in a bucket, When push come to shove, West L.A. fadeaway, Tons of steel, Throwing stones, Black muddy river.
(Arista AL 8452. Release date, July 6th, 1987).
Only cassette version includes My brother Esau.
BUILT TO LAST - Foolish heart, Just a little light, Victim or the crime, Standing on the moon, Blow away, Picasso moon, Built to last, I will take you home.

(Arista 8575. Release date October 31st, 1989).
Only CD and cassette version includes We can run.
WITHOUT A NET - Feel like a stranger, Mississippi half-step uptown toodeloo, Walkin' blues, Althea, Cassidy, Let it grow, China cat sunflower, I know you rider, Looks like rain, Eyes of the world, Victim or the crime, Help on the way, Slipknot!, Franklin's tower, Bird song, One more saturday night, Dear Mr. Fantasy.
(Arista AL3-8634. Release date September 1990. Triple live)
ONE FROM THE VAULT - Introduction, Help on the way, Franklin's tower, The music never stopped, It must have been the roses, Eyes of the world, Drums, King Solomon's marbles, Around & around, Sugaree, Big river, Crazy fingers, Drums, The other one, Sage and spirit, Goin' down the road feeling bad, U.S. blues, Blues for Allah.
(Grateful Dead GDCD40132. Release date July 1991. Double CD recorded live at the Great American Music Hall, San Francisco, on August 13, 1975)
INFRARED ROSES - I: Crowd sculpture, Parallelogram, Little Nemo in nightland. II: Riverside rhapsody, Post-modern highrise table top stomp, Infrared roses. III: Silver apples of the moon, Speaking in swords, Magnesium night light. IV: Sparrow hawk row, River of nine sorrows, Apollo at the Ritz.
(Grateful Dead GDCD40142. Release date December 1991. Double live CD)
TWO FROM THE VAULT - Good morning little schoolgirl, Dark star, Saint Stephen, The eleven, Death don't have no mercy, The other one, New potatoe caboose, Turn on your lovelight, Morning dew.
(Grateful Dead GDCD40162. Release date May 1992. Recorded live at Shrine Aditorium, Los Angeles, August 23/24, 1968)

ANTHOLOGIES

VINTAGE DEAD - Good morning little schoolgirl, Lindy, Stealin', The same thing.
(Sunflower SUN 5001. Recorded live at the Avalon Ballroom in 1966. Released date 1970)
HISTORIC DEAD - I know you rider, It hurts me too, It's all over now baby blue, Dancin' in the streets, In the midnight hour.
(MGM/Sunflower SNF 5004. Recorded live at the Avalon Ballroom in 1966. Release date 1971)
POP HISTORY 13 - German release includes some Dead tracks.
(Polydor, 1972)
POP HISTORY 23 - German release includes some Dead tracks.
(Polydor, 1972)
HISTORY OF THE GRATEFUL DEAD (VOLUME ONE): BEAR'S CHOICE - Katie Mae, Dark hollow, I've been all around this world, Wake up little Susie, Black Peter, Smokestack Lightnin', Hard to handle.
(Warner Bros. BS 2721. Release date July 13, 1973. Recorded live at Fillmore East, NYC, February 10/11/13/14, 1970)
THE HISTORY OF THE GRATEFUL DEAD
A "Best" of the *Vintage Dead* and *Historic Dead* albums.
(Pride PRD 0016. Release date, 1973)
SKELETONS FROM THE CLOSET/THE BEST OF THE GRATEFUL DEAD - The golden road (to unlimited devotion), Truckin', Rosemary, Sugar Magnolia, St. Stephen, Uncle John's band, Casey Jones, Mexicali blues, Turn on your lovelight, One more saturday night, Friend of the devil.
(Warner Bros. W 2764. Release date 1974)
WHAT A LONG STRANGE TRIP IT'S BEEN - New, new Minglewood blues, Cosmic Charlie, Truckin', Black Peter, Born cross-eyed, Ripple, Doin' that rag, Dark star, High time, New speedway boogie, St. Stephen, Jack straw, Me and my uncle,

Tennessee Jed, Cumberland blues, Playing in the band, Brown-eyed woman, Ramble on rose.
(Warner Bros. 2W 3091. Release date July 1977)
SUPERSTARS OF THE 70s VOL. 2 - Compilation including Johnny B. Goode from the *Grateful Dead* release.
(Warner Special Products, 1987)
ARISTA's PERFECT 10 RIDES AGAIN - Includes Alabama getaway.
(Arista, 1987)
DEAD ZONE - Limited edition box set with booklet. Contains the CD edition of *Terrapin Station, Shakedown Street, Go to heaven, Reckoning, Dead set, In the dark.*
(Arista. Release date 1988)
AA.VV.: "DEADICATED" - Bertha, Jack straw, U.S. blues, Ship of fools, China doll, Cassidy, Truckin', Casey Jones, Uncle John's band, Friend of the devil, To lay me down, Wharf rat, Estimated prophet, Deal, Ripple.
(Arista ARCD 8669. Release date 1991. Various artists tribute to Grateful Dead)

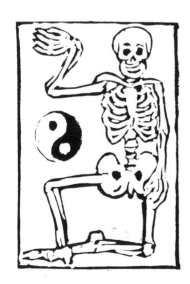

PROMOTIONAL & RADIO SHOWS

WARNER/REPRISE RECORD SHOW *(Warner Bros. PRO 289, 1969)*

THE BIG BALL *(Warner Bros., 1969)*

LOONEY TUNES AND MERRIE MELODIES *(Warner Bros. PRO 423, 1970)*

AMERICAN BEAUTY, 7" promo single *(Warner Bros., 1970)*

AMERICAN BEAUTY promo EP *(Warner Bros. 1970)*

ARMED FORCES RADIO SHOW *(AFRTS RL3-2, 1972)*

THE WHOLE BURBANK CATALOG *(Warner Bros. PRO512, 1972)*

BURBANK *(Warner Bros., 1972)*

ARMED FORCES RADIO SHOW *(AFRTS 26, 1972)*

EUROPE '72 promo EP *(Warner Bros. 1972)*

JOHNNY B. GOODE/SO FINE, promo single with Elvin Bishop Group on the B-side *(Warner Bros., 1972)*

RAMBLE ON ROSE/JACK STRAW AND MR. CHARLY, promo single from *Europe '72 (Warner Bros, 1972)*

SAMPLER FOR DEAD HEADS, Hunter/Garcia *(Round, 1974)*

LET IT ROCK, promo single from *Compliments of... (Round, 1974)*

RUM RUNNERS, promo single from *Tales of... (Round, 1974)*

U.S. BLUES, promo single *(Grateful Dead, 1974)*

SAMPLER FOR DEAD HEADS, Old & in the way/ Keith-Donna Godchaux *(Round 1975)*

SAMPLER FOR DEAD HEADS, Robert Hunter/Phil Lesh & Ned Lagin *(Round 1975)*

FOR DEAD HEADS *(United Artists 1975)*

THE MUSIC NEVER STOPPED, promo single *(UA GD, 1975)*

FRANKLIN'S TOWER, promo single *(UA GD, 1975)*

GRATEFUL DEAD SAMPLER *(Arista 1977)*

THE ANNIVERSARY ALBUM *(Warner Bros 1977)*

RECENTLY DEAD *(Arista 1977)*

PASSENGER, promo single *(Arista, 1977)*

DANCIN' IN THE STREETS, promo single *(Arista, 1977)*

I'LL BE DOGGONE, promo single from *Heaven help... (Arista, 1977)*

CALIFORNIA EARTHQUAKE, live single of Rodney Crowell's 1978 song

GOOD LOVIN', promo single *(Arista, 1978)*

SHAKEDOWN STREET, promo single *(Arista, 1978)*

KING BISCUIT FLOWER HOUR, Nassau Coliseum Show *(King Biscuit 1980)*

KING BISCUIT FLOWER HOUR, a retrospective of various '70s shows *(King Biscuit 198)*

EARTH NEWS RADIO *(1980)*

EARTH NEWS RADIO SPECIAL *(Earth News Radio 1980)*

ROCK'N'ROLL VALENTINE *(Westwood One, 1981)*

THE GRATEFUL DEAD STORY, Dec. 20, 1981

ROCK'N'ROLL NEVER FORGETS *(ABC/DIR, 1981)*

OFF THE RECORD WITH MARY TURNER *(1981)*

ROCK AND ROLL VALENTINE *(Westwood One 1981)*

SPECIAL SOURCE *(Special Source 1981)*

KING BISCUIT FLOWER HOUR, February 5, 1982 *(King Biscuit)*

THE WHITE EP-JOE POP-O PIE *(415 A0009, 1982)*

RSMP GUEST DJ's *(1982)*

FOR THE FAITHFUL, special package by a subsidiary of Arista Record of 'Reckoning'. *(Pair Records 1984)*

ARISTA'S GREATEST AOR HITS: PORTRAIT OF A DECADE 1975-1985 *(Arista, 1985)*

WHAT KEEPS THE DEAD ALIVE? *(Westwood One 1985)*

SERIES 17 AND 19: JIM LADD INTERVIEW SERIES

DEAD IN A DECK, picture CD edition of *Built to last*. The box set includes a card deck drawn by Rick Griffin. *(Arista 1987)*

TOUCH OF GREY, grey vinyl promo with mini poster. *(Arista 1987)*

GRATEFUL DEAD TALK TO THEMSELVES *(Arista ADP-9630, 1987)*

TOUCH OF GRAY/TOUCH OF GRAY, promo single *(Arista, 1987)*

TOUCH OF GRAY/MY BROTHER ESAU, promo 12"

(Arista, 1987)
HELL IN A BUCKET/WEST L.A. FADEAWAY, promo 12" (Arista, 1987)
THROWING STONES (ASHES ASHES), promo 12" (Arista, 1988)
LIBERTY, Hunter's promo single (Relix, 1988)
GRATEFUL DEAD (Legends of rock 1988)
KING BISCUIT FLOWER HOUR: THE GRATEFUL DEAD Pt. 1 (King Biscuit, 1988)
ROCKSTARS No. 15: THE GRATEFUL DEAD (RTE, 1988)
RARITIES RADIO SHOW (RTE, 1988)
MONTEREY POP RADIO SPECIAL (1988)
BOB DYLAN & GRATEFUL DEAD, picture promo of the album with the same title (Columbia 1989)
GRATEFUL DEAD 'ANTE UP', promo album containing 'Built to last' plus an interview. (Arista 1989)
GRATEFUL DEAD '1989 Part 1 & 2', Up Close Music and Interview. Radio Show, 4 CD
GRATEFUL DEAD 'DEAD ON ARRIVAL', November 20th, 1989, 2 LPs + interview (Rock Stars Music)
BUILT TO LAST, promo album with nine tracks (Arista 1989)
FOOLISH HART/WE CAN RUN, promo CD single (Arista, 1989)
FOOLISH HART, promotional CD single with insert (Arista ASCD 1989)
GRATEFUL DEAD HOUR No. 1/87, a weekly one hour show by David Gams (Truth and Fun Inc. 1988/1990)
THE HEART OF ROCK (Columbia, 1989)
UP CLOSE WITH THE GRATEFUL DEAD (Media America, 1989)
TIMOTHY WHITE'S ROCK STARS - THE GRATEFUL DEAD (Westwood One, 1989)
LIVE - Vol. 1 - CLASSIC ROCK FROM THE 60's and 70's (Warner Special Products, 1989)
IN THE MIDNIGHT HOUR/DEAD DON'T HAVE NO MERCY, live 33 rpm 7" inserted in the italian Ripple magazine Vol. 1 Dead 1 (Koiné, 1989)
HIGH TIME/CUMBERLAND BLUES, live 33 rpm 7" inserted in the italian Ripple magazine Vol. 1 Dead

2 (Wild Bird, 1990)
SOUNDS OF THE SEVENTIES (Time-Life Books, 1990)
WITHOUT A NET, limited edition in picture CD of the same album. Special cardboard including a Rick Griffin's poster (Arista 1990)
GRATEFUL DEAD DECEMBER 9, 1990 (King Biscuit)
DEADICATED EXTRA (Up Close 1991)
GRATEFUL DEAD (Up Close 1991)
GRATEFUL DEAD DECEMBER 16, 1991 (King Biscuit)
GRATEFUL DEAD DECEMBER 22, 1991 (King Biscuit)

SOLO DISCOGRAPHIES

JERRY GARCIA

HOOTEROLL?
(Douglas KZ 30859. Release date 1971. By Howard Wales and Jerry Garcia)
GARCIA *(Warner Bros. BS 2582. Release date January 1972)*
LIVE AT THE KEYSTONE
(Fantasy F 79002. By Merl Saunders, Jerry Garcia, John Kahn, Bill Vitt. Release date 1973)
COMPLIMENTS OF GARCIA
(Round Records RX 102. Release date June 1st, 1974)
OLD AND IN THE WAY
(Round Records RX 103. Release date March 1975. Old and in the Way featuring Jerry Garcia)
REFLECTIONS
(Round Records RX 107/United Artists LA 565 G. Release date January 1976)
CATS UNDER THE STARS
(Arista AB 4160. Jerry Garcia Band. Release date April 1978)
RUN FOR THE ROSES
(Arista AL 9603. Release date 1982)
KEYSTONE ENCORES VOL. 1
(Fantasy MPF 4533. By Merl Saunders, Jerry Garcia, John Kahn, Bill Vitt. Release date 1988)
KEYSTONE ENCORES VOL. 2
(Fantasy MPF 4534. By Merl Saunders, Jerry Garcia, John Kahn, Bill Vitt. Release date 1988)
ALMOST ACOUSTIC
(Concensus GDCD/Reality 4005/Grateful Dead Records GDDLP 5.00036 M. Release date December 1988. Single and double live album with the Jerry Garcia Band)
JERRY GARCIA BAND
(Arista 18690-2. Release date Fall 1991. Recorded live during 1990. 2 CD set)

JERRY GARCIA/DAVID GRISMAN
(Acoustic Disc ACD-2. Release date Fall 1991)

BOB WEIR

ACE
(Warner Bros. BS 2627. Release date January 1972)
KINGFISH
(Round RX 108/United Artists LA 564 G. Kingfish featuring Bob Weir. Release date March 1976)
LIVE 'N KICKIN'
(Jet JT LA 732/United Artists G. By Kingfish featuring Bob Weir. Release date 1977)
HEAVEN HELP THE FOOL
(Arista AB 4155. By Bob Weir Band. Release date 1977)
BOBBY AND THE MIDNITES
(Arista AL 9568. By Bobby and the Midnites. Release date November 1981)
WHERE THE BEATS MEETS THE STREET
(Columbia BFC 39276. By Bobby and the Midnites. Release date November 1984)
KINGFISH
(Relix RRLP 2005. Release date 1985)

MICKEY HART

ROLLING THUNDER
(Warner Bros. BS 2335. Release date May 1972)
DIGA
(Round RX 110/United Artists LA 600 G. Release date March 1976)
APOCALYPSE NOW
(Elektra DP 90001. Release date 1979. Original motion picture soundtrack featuring Mickey Hart, Bill Kreutzmann and Phil Lesh)
THE APOCALYPSE NOW SESSION/THE RHYTM DEVILS PLAY RIVER MUSIC
(Passport PB 9844. By The Rhytm Devils, featuring Mickey Hart, Bill Kreutzmann and Phil Lesh. Release date 1980)

YAMANTAKA
(Celestial Harmonies CEL 003. By Henry Wolf, Nancy Hennings and Mickey Hart. Release date 1983)
MUSIC TO BE BORN BY
(Rykodisc RCD 20112/RACS. Release date April 1989)
DAFOS
(Ryko RCD 10108/RACS; also available on Reference Recordings RR-12. By Mickey Hart, Airto Moreira, Flora Purim. Release date 1989)
AT THE EDGE
(Rykodisc RCD 10124. Release date 1990)

PHIL LESH

SEASTONES - A union of music biology and physics.
(Round Records RX 106. By Phil Lesh and Ned Lagin. Release date January 1975)

KEITH and DONNA GODCHAUX

KEITH & DONNA
(Round Records RX 104. Release date, March 1975)
THE GHOSTS PLAYING IN THE HEART OF GOLD BAND
(Whirled WRR 01967. Release date 1984)
THE HEART OF GOLD BAND
(Relix RRLP 2020. Release date 1986)

TOM CONSTANTEN

TAROT/TOCHSTONE
(United Artists UAS 5563. Release date 1972)
FRESH TRACKS IN REAL TIME
(Tom Constanten private production. Available only on tape. Release date 1990)
NIGHTFALL OF DIAMONDS
(Relix Records RR CD 2046. Release date 1992)

BRENT MYDLAND

SILVER
(Arista AL 4076. Release date 1976)

ROBERT HUNTER

TALES OF THE GREAT RUM RUNNERS
(Round Records RX 101. Release date 1974)
TIGER ROSE
(Round Records RX 105. Release date 1975)
JACK O' ROSES
(Relix Records RRLP 2001. Release date 1981)
PROMONTORY RIDER
(Relix Records RRLP 2002. Release date 1982)
AMAGAMALIN STREET
(Relix Records RRLP 2003. Release date 1984)
LIVE 1985
(Relix Records RRLP 2006. Release date 1985)
THE FLIGHT OF THE MARIE HELENA
(Relix Records RRLP 2009. Release date 1985)
ROCK COLUMBIA
(Relix Records RRLP 2019. Release date 1986)
LIBERTY
(Relix Records RRLP 2029. Release date 1987)
DINOSAURS
(Relix Records RRLP 2031. Release date 1988. By The Dinosaurs, featuring Robert Hunter)
A BOX OF RAIN
(Rykodisc RCD 10214. Release date 1991. Recorded live during 1990)

GRATEFUL DEAD SINGLES

(Warlox) The emergency crew
(Autumn Records. 1965)
Don't ease me in/Stealin'
(Scorpio 201. June 1966)
The golden road (to unlimited devotion)/Cream puff war *(Warner Bros. 7016. March 17th, 1967)*
Fire in the city/Your sons and daughters *(circa 1967)*, used for the John Hendricks' movie.
Dark star/Born cross-eyed
(Warner Bros. WB 7186. April 1968)
Dupree's diamond blues/Cosmic Charlie
(Warner Bros. WB 7324. June 20th, 1969)
Uncle John's Band/New speedway boogie
(Warner Bros. 7410. May 1970)
Truckin'/Ripple
(Warner Bros. 7464. November 1970)
Johnny B. Goode/Truckin' *(Warner Bros. 1972)*
Bertha/One more saturday night
(Warner Bros. 1972)
Sugar Magnolia/Mr. Charlie
(Warner Bros. 7667. 1972)
Casey Jones/Keep your lamps trimmed and burning (side B Hot Tuna), italian release from *The last days of the Fillmore* LP *(Int. Sir., 1972)*
Truckin'/Sugar Magnolia
(Warner Bros. 7-21988)
Let me sing your blues away/Here comes sunshine *(Grateful Dead Records GDS-01. October 15th, 1973)*
Eyes of the world/Weather report Part. I
(Grateful Dead Records GDS-4502. 1973)
U. S. Blues/Loose Lucy
(Grateful Dead Records GDS-4503. June 27th, 1974)
The music never stopped/Franklin's tower
(United Artists GD 718. September 1st, 1975)
Help on the way/Franklin's tower
(United Artists GD 762. 1975)

Dancin' in the streets/Terrapin Station
(Arista 0276. July 27th, 1977)
Dancin' in the streets/Terrapin Station, UK release
(Arista Dead-1)
Passenger/Terrapin Station
(Arista 0291. 1977)
Dark star/Born cross-eyed
(Dark Star. 1977)
Dancin' in the streets/Terrapin Station
(Arista 1972-0276. 1977, July 27)
Passenger/Terrapin Station
(Arista 0291. 1977, July 27)
Good lovin'/Stagger Lee
(Arista 0383. November 15th, 1978)
Shakedown Street/France
(Arista 0410. 1978)
Alabama getaway/Far from me
(Arista 0519. April 28th, 1980)
Don't ease me in/Far from me
(Arista 0546. 1980)
Alabama getaway/Shakedown Street *(Arista. 1981)*
Touch of gray/My brother Esau, grey vinyl with poster *(Arista AS1-9606. June 16th, 1987)*
Touch of gray/My brother Esau, CD single *(Arista ASCD-9606. 1987)*
Touch of gray/My brother Esau, black vinyl single *(Arista AS1-9606. 1987)*
Touch of gray/My brother Esau,
UK release *(Arista Rist.-35. 1987)*
Touch of gray/My brother Esau
(Arista. 1987. Tape single)
In the dark
(Arista. 1987. Interview)
Throwing stones (Ashes ashes)/Push comes to shove *(Arista AS1-9643. January 1988)*
Touch of gray/Throwing stones (ashes ashes) *(Arista Flash AFS9686. 1988)*
Foolish heart/We can run, CD single *(Arista ASCD 9899. October 12, 1989)*
Foolish heart/We can run, cassette single with 5 cards *(Arista 9899. October 12, 1989)*
Foolish heart/We can run
(Arista AS1-9899. 1989)

SOLO SINGLES

JERRY GARCIA

Uncle Martin's/South Side strut
(Douglas ZS7-6501. By Howard Wales and Jerry Garcia. 1971)
Deal/The wheel *(Warner Bros WB 7551. Jan. 1972)*
Sugaree/Eep hour *(Warner Bros. WB 7569. 1972)*
Let it rock/Midnight town
(Round Records RX 4504. June 21st, 1974)

BOB WEIR

One more saturday night/Cassidy
(Warner Bros. WB 7611. 1972)
Bombs away/Easy to sleep *(Arista 0315. 1977)*

MICKEY HART

Blind John/Pump song
(Warner Bros. WB 7644. 1972)
3 Inches of the world, CD single *(Rykodisk RCD3)*

ROBERT HUNTER

Rum runners/It must have been the roses
(Round Records RX 4505. 1974)
It must have been the roses/It must have been the roses *(Round Records promo single. 1974)*
Aim at the heart/Who, baby, who?
(Relix Records RR 451. 1986)

BRENT MYDLAND

Wham bam shang a lang
From the Silver's album *(Arista, 1976)*

PARTICIPATIONS

KEN KESEY - The acid trip
(Sound City, 1967)
JEFFERSON AIRPLANE - Surrealistic pillow
(RCA, 1967)
JEFFERSON AIRPLANE - Volunteers
(RCA, 1969) (Garcia)
VV.AA. - The 1969 Warner Reprise Record Set
(Warner Bros, 1969). Anthology with Grateful Dead.
JEFFERSON AIRPLANE - The worst of J.A.
(RCA 1970) (Garcia)
VV.AA. - Zabriskie Point
(MGM, 1970). Soundtrack of the movie by Michelangelo Antonioni. A track by Grateful Dead *(Dark star)* and one by Garcia alone *(Love scene)*. The later is no available elsewhere.
PAUL KANTNER/JEFFERSON STARSHIP - Blows against the empire
(RCA, 1970) (Garcia, Hart, Kreutzmann)
CROSBY, STILLS, NASH & YOUNG - Deja vu
(Atlantic, 1970) (Garcia)
IT'S A BEAUTIFUL DAY - Marrying Maiden
(Columbia, 1970) (Garcia)
INCREDIBLE STRING BAND - U
(Elektra, 1970) (Tom Constanten)
BREWER & SHIPLEY - Tarkio
(Kama Sutra, 1970) (Garcia)
PAUL KANTNER/GRACE SLICK - Sunfighter
(Grunt, 1971) (Garcia, Kreutzmann)
DAVID CROSBY - If I could only remember my name *(Atlantic, 1971)*
(Garcia, Lesh, Hart, Kreutzman)
GRAHAM NASH - Song for beginners
(Atlantic, 1971) (Garcia)
NEW RIDERS OF THE PURPLE SAGE - NRPS
(Columbia, 1971) (Garcia, Lesh, Hart)
PAPA JOHN CREACH - Papa John Creach
(Grunt, 1971) (Garcia)

JAMES AND THE GOOD BROTHERS - Same
(Columbia, 1971) (Garcia)
STEPHEN STILLS - 2 *(Atlantic, 1971)* (Garcia)
LAMB - Cross between
(Warner Bros., 1971) (Garcia)
MERL SAUNDERS - Heavy Turbulence
(Fantasy, 1972) (Garcia)
VV.AA. - Fillmore: the last days
(Columbia/Fillmore, 1972)
(Triple album set with all Frisco people. Grateful
Dead plays *Casey Jones* and *Johnny B. Goode*)
VV.AA. Glastonbury Fayre Festival
(Revelation, 1972)
(Triple album set from the U.K. festival. There's an
extraordinaire *Dark star* of over 26 min.)
NEW RIDERS OF THE PURPLE SAGE - Powerglide
(Columbia, 1972) (Garcia, Kreutzmann)
TOM FOGERTY - Tom Fogerty
(Fantasy, 1972) (Garcia)
DAVID BROMBERG - Demon in disguise
(Columbia, 1972) (Garcia, Lesh, Kreutzmann,
Godchaux)
CROSBY & NASH - David Crosby and Graham Nash
(Atlantic, 1972) (Garcia, Lesh, Kreutzmann)
CHRIS & LORIN ROWAN - Rowan Brothers
(Columbia, 1972) (Garcia, Kreutzmann)
NEW RIDERS OF THE PURPLE SAGE - Gipsy cowboy
(Columbia, 1972) (Keith & Donna Godchaux)
MERL SAUNDERS - Fire up
(Fantasy, 1973) (Garcia)
PAUL KANTNER/GRACE SLICK/DAVID FREIBERG -
Baron Von Tollbooth and the Chrome Nun
(Grunt, 1973) (Garcia, Hart)
LINK WRAY - Be what you want to
(Polydor, 1973)
ART GARFUNKEL - Angel clare
(Columbia, 1973) (Garcia)
DAVID REA and SLEWFOOT -
(CBS/Windfall, 1973) (Garcia, Weir, Godchaux)
TOM FOGERTY - Excalibur
(Fantasy, 1973) (Garcia)
NEW RIDERS OF THE PURPLE SAGE - The adventures
Panama Red

(Columbia, 1973) (Donna Godchaux)
DAVID BROMBERG - Wanted dead or alive
(Columbia, 1974) (Garcia, Lesh, Kreutzmann)
NEW RIDERS OF THE PURPLE SAGE - Oh, what a...
(Columbia, 1975) (Garcia)
KENTUCKY COLONELS - Livin' in the past
(Briar, 1975) (Garcia)
QUICKSILVER MESSENGER SERVICE - Solid silver
(Capitol, 1975) (Hunter)
JEFFERSON STARSHIP - Red octopus
(Grunt, 1975) (Hunter)
ERIC ANDERSEN - Sweet surprise
(Arista, 1976) (Brent Mydland)
THE GOOD OLD BOYS - Pistol-Packin' *(Round,
1976)* (Garcia)
BARRY MELTON - The fish
(United Artists, 1976) (Hunter/Hart)
NORTON BUFFALO - Loving in the valley of the
moon
(Capitol, 1977) (Hart)
NORTON BUFFALO - Desert horizon
(Capitol, 1977) (Hart)
ROWAN BROS. - Jubilation
(Asylum, 1977) (Hart)
HAMZA EL DIN - Eclipse
(Pacific Arts Records, 1979) (Hart)
LITTLE FEAT - Down on the farm
(Warner Bros., 1979) (K. Godchaux)
VV.AA. - MORE AMERICAN GRAFFITI
(1979) Includes *Cream puff war* (Grateful Dead)
CROSBY, STILLS & NASH - Replay
(Atlantic, 1980) (Garcia)
PETER ROWAN - Txican Badman
(Appaloosa, 1980) (Garcia, Kreutzmann)
CRIS & LORIN ROWAN - Livin' the life
(Appaloosa, 1980) (Garcia, Kreutzmann)
VV.AA. - The waltz project
(Elektra, 1981) (Tom Constanten)
VV.AA. - Rock southern style
(KTEL, 1982) (Grateful Dead)
THE ELECTRIC GUITAR QUARTET - Same
(EGQ, 1983) (Tom Constanten. Personal
production, tape only)

VV.AA. - Mask
(MCA, 1984) (Grateful Dead)
RELIX RECORD SAMPLER #1
(Relix, 1985) (Hunter)
THE BEST OF/DIRE WOLF
Release from *Workingman's dead*
(Platinum, 1985)
NEW RIDERS OF THE PURPLE SAGE - Before time began
(Relix, 1986) (Garcia, Lesh, Hart. Studio 1969/70)
MATT KELLY - A wing and a prayer
(Relix, 1986) (Garcia, Weir, Godchaux, Mydland)
VV.AA. - The digital domain: a demonstration
(Elektra/Asylum CD, 1986) (Hart)
NEVILLE BROTHERS - Uptown
(EPI-America/Rounder, 1987) (Garcia)
NEW RIDERS OF THE PURPLE SAGE - Vintage
(Relix, 1987) (Garcia. Live 1970)
KITARO - The light of the spirit
(Geffen, 1987) (Hart)
NEGATIVLAND - Escape from noise
(SST, 1987) (Garcia/Hart/Mydland)
ZAHIR HUSSAIN - s/t
(Aspen Records, 1987) (Hart)
ORNETTE COLEMAN - Virgin beauty
(CBS, 1988) (Garcia)
COUNTRY JOE - Peace on heart
(Ragbaby Records, 1988) (Hart/Weir)
PETE SEARS - Watchfire
(Redweed Records, 1988) (Garcia/Hart)
BRIAN MELVIN - Nightfood
(Weir)
BOB DYLAN - Dylan & The Dead
(Columbia, 1989) (Grateful Dead)
BOB DYLAN - Down in the groove
(Columbia, 1989) (Grateful Dead)
MERL SAUNDERS - Blues for the rainforest
(Summertone Records 1990) (Garcia)
THE OBSEQUIOUS CHEESE LONG - If six was nine
(Imaginary Rec., 1990) (Weir)
THE HENRY KAISER BAND - Heart's desire
(Reckless, 1990) (Tom Constanten)
VV.AA. - Greenpeace 'Rainbow Warriors'

(CDGP 9, 1990) (Benefit compilation for Greenpeace. The Dead are present with *Throwing Stones*)
WARREN ZEVON - Transverse city
(Virgin, 1990) (Garcia)
COUNTRY JOE - Superstitious blues
(Rykodisc, 1991) (Garcia)
KEN NORDINE - Devot catalyst
(Grateful Dead, 1992) (Garcia)
BOB WASSERMAN - Trios
(to be released) (Garcia)

BOOTLEGRAPHY (LP)

In alphabetical order

ACOUSTIC DEAD
(Berkeley 6969) FM live concert 1971 w/New Riders of the Purple Sage; insert. 1 LP USA
ACOUSTIC DEAD
(Black Gold BG 6969) Same above with a deluxe red and white cover. 1 LP USA
AIN'T IT CRAZY
(Apocalypse 743-WCF) Live 1971. 1 LP USA
AIN'T IT CRAZY
(Sugar Magnolia Rec. SMR 743) same above. 1 LP USA
ANDERSON THEATRE 1970
New York City Nov. 11, 1970; with deluxe purple & black cover. 600 numbered copies, first 20 in coloured vinyl. 1 LP EEC.
A SWELL DANCE CONCERT
(Toasted Record Works TRW 1918) New Year's show 1987; deluxe cover. 2 LP USA
BEACH BOYS MEET THE GRATEFUL DEAD
(BBGD) Fillmore East, New York City Apr. 27, 1971. 2 LP USA
BEST OF GRATEFUL DEAD
1 LP EEC
BOX OF RAIN
(Berkeley Records) Live 1972. 1 LP USA
BRIDGET'S ALBUM
(Pharting Pharoah 13163) Eugene, Oregon July 19, 1987 w/Bob Dylan; deluxe colour cover. 2 LP USA
BROKEDOWN PALACE
April 8, 1985, Spectrum Philadelphia. Deluxe colour cover. 2 LP USA
BY THE TIME WE GOT TO WOODSTOCK
(M 161) Woodstock Festival Aug. 16, 1969. Deluxe brown & white cover; 300 copies on clear vinyl. 1 LP EEC

BY THE TIME WE GOT TO WOODSTOCK
(MGLAB) Same above. 1 LP EEC
CAPTAIN TRIPS, ETC.
(Impossible Record Works 1-33) Hollywood Palladium, New York City 1969. Deluxe black & white cover. 1 LP USA
CENTRAL PARK, FILLMORE EAST, ACTION HOUSE
(Berkeley 2233) Central Park, New York City June 22, 1969 + Action House, Long Island Nov. 11, 1970 + Fillmore East, May 1970. 1 LP USA
COMES ALIVE
(Unicorn Music UM45AG) New York City Oct. 1980. Deluxe colour cover. 2 LP USA
CONCERTS THAT ROCK THE WORLD VOLUME 1
300 copies colored vinyl. 1 LP EEC
CONCERTS THAT ROCK THE WORLD VOLUME 1
200 copies. 1 LP EEC
CONCERTS THAT ROCK THE WORLD VOLUME 1
Unlimited. 1 LP EEC
COSMIC DEATH
(FB 125) Madison Feb. 1973. Deluxe colour cover. 1 LP EEC
COSMIC SEVEN
feat. Carlos Santana. 2 LP EEC
COSMIK MESSENGERS
(UFCS Records CSR 003) Stony Brook, New York City Oct. 30, 1970; second show. Deluxe red & blue cover, deluxe label. 1 LP USA
COWBOY'S DEAD
(Sugar Magnolia Rec. SMR 803) Harpur College, Bringhampton May 2, 1970. 1 LP USA
CRAZY FINGERS
(Amazing Stork Rec. ASR 7483) Palais de Seine, Paris Sept. 20/22, 1974. Deluxe colored cover with deluxe label. 2 LP USA
(THE) CRYPTICAL ENVELOPMENT
(RSR/International RSR 237) Deluxe colored cover; B/W back. 2 LP EEC
DANCING SKELETON
(MEL 78 L 28192) Picture, 2000 copies. 1 LP USA
DARK STAR
(Berkeley 2255) FM live broadcast 1971, with insert. 1 LP USA

DARK STAR
(Impossible Record Works 2255) Deluxe B/W cover; same above. 1 LP USA
DEAD AHEAD
(ATT GD 102680) Tempe Oct. 6, 1977 + Passaic Nov. 24, 1978 + Nassau Coliseum Feb 5th, 1980. 2 LP USA
DEAD RELIX
(Dog'n'Cats Rec. WRMB 517) Oakland Oct. 10, 1976. 1 LP USA
DEADER THAN DOORNAILS
(TDIC Recs) See "Dire Wolf". 1 LP USA
DEAD/LIVE
(Berkeley 2001/2002) 2 LP USA
DEAD NON STOP - 2 LP USA
DIRE WOLF
(Berkeley 2036) Fillmore East Apr. 1971 + El Monte CA Dec. 1970. 1 LP USA
DON'T EASE ME IN
200 copies. 1 LP USA
DOUBLE DEAD
(PQ 401) Side 1 same as S1 of "Silent Dead"/Side 2 same as S2 of "Silent Dead"/ Side 3 same as S1 of "Felt Forum 1971"/Side 4 same as S2 of "Felt Forum 1971". The order of the songs on Side 1 is uncorrected on the cover. 2 LP USA
EASY RIDERS
June 30, 1987, Toronto, Canada. Deluxe colour cover. 2 LP USA
(THE) ELECTRIC KOOL-AID ACID TEST
(UFCS Records SMS 001) San Francisco State College Oct. 1st/2nd, 1966. Deluxe red & blue cover; deluxe label. 1 LP USA
EUROPEAN TOUR 1974
UK & France 1974. Deluxe B/W cover. Cover has songs out of order. 2 LP USA
FAREWELL TO WINTERLAND
(LAX 1698) Winterland, San Francisco Dec. 31, 1978 w/J. Cipollina, L. Oscar, M. Kelly, Ken Kesey, Ken Babbs & Merry Pranksters. Deluxe B/W cover. 3 LP USA
FAREWELL TO WINTERLAND
Picture disc, same above. 1 LP USA

FELT FORUM 1971
(Berkeley 101) New York City Dec. 5, 1971. 1 LP USA
FELT FORUM 1971
(CBM J) Same above. 1 LP USA
FELT FORUM 1971
(Sugar Magnolia Rec. A 101) Same above. 1 LP USA
FILLMORE WEST
(HH Dead Fillmore) FM broadcast 'The last days at Fillmore West', San Francisco July 3rd, 1971. 2 LP USA
FILLMORE WEST
(TMOQ 72014) Same above. 2 LP USA
FILLMORE WEST
(TMOQ 72014) Coloured vinyl, same above. 2 LP USA
FOR DEAD HEADS ONLY
(Poow Productions) Winterland, San Francisco, New Year's Eve 70/71 + Felt Forum, New York 1971 + Capitol Theatre Aug. 26th, 1978. 3 LP Box set USA
FRANKLIN'S TOWER
(FB 131) San Francisco Aug. 13rd, 1975. 1 LP EEC
FRESHLY DEAD IN '66
(Bewitching Music Inc.) Side 1 Los Angeles Jan. 1966; side 2 tracks 1-6 Fillmore Auditorium San Francisco July 3rd, 1966.
Two tracks of Jorma Kaukonen on side two. Deluxe colour cover. 2 LP USA
FRESHLY DEAD IN L.A. & S.F.
Same above. 2 LP EEC
GARCIA'S GANG
(Fugitive Records 63-67) Fillmore East New York City Apr. 26/27/28, 1971; w/Duane Allman. Deluxe B/W cover. Red lettering. 2 LP USA
GOD LOVIN'
(Smilin' Ears 77-401) Englishtown Sep. 3, 1977 + Fillmore West SF July 2nd, 1971. Deluxe box set. 4 LP USA
GRATEFUL DEAD
(Dark Star Rec. GD 2255)
With insert. 1 LP USA

GRATEFUL DEAD
(Fabbri) Studio + live tracks from Europe '72. Released only on tape. 1 MC EEC
GRATEFUL DEAD
(Fade Records GD 2222) With insert. 1 LP USA
GRATEFUL DEAD
(HHCER 103) Circa 1972. 1 LP USA
GRATEFUL DEAD
(GD 2233) Action House, New York City Nov. 11, 1970. With insert. 1 LP USA
GRATEFUL DEAD
(International 202)
Glastonbury Fayre Festival 1971 + studio '66. 1 LP USA
GRATEFUL DEAD
(Sugar Magnolia Rec. 2222) 1 LP USA
GRATEFUL DEAD
(Sugaree GD 2244) With insert. 1 LP USA
GRATEFUL DEAD
(THC Production 101) With insert. 1 LP USA
GRATEFUL DEAD
2 LP USA
GRATEFUL DEAD
New York Sept. 24th, 1988 w/Mick Taylor and Suzanne Vega. 1 LP EEC
GRATEFUL DEAD FOOL'S DAY
3 LP EEC
GRATEFUL DEAD, STONYBROOK
Hofstra University Oct. 30th, 1970. 1 LP USA
HEAD TRIP
(79-148/149/150/151 M) Portland Oct. 2, 1977 + St. Louis Feb. 11, 1979 + Passaic, Nov. 24, 1978 + Red Rocks July 7, 1978. 2 LP USA
HIGH TIME IN THE OLD TOWN
(CBM 1020) Chicago Auditorium Oct. 21, 1971. 1 LP USA
HIGHWAY DEAD
(HHCER 103) 1 LP USA
HOLLYWOOD PALLADIUM 1
(TMOQ 7164) Live 1971. 1 LP USA
HOLLYWOOD PALLADIUM
(TMOQ 71064) Same above. Colored vinyl. 1 LP USA

HOLLYWOOD PALLADIUM
(Berkeley 2003) Same above. 1 LP USA
HOLLYWOOD PALLADIUM 2
(TMOQ 72008) Also available as "Out West". 2 LP USA
HOLLYWOOD PALLADIUM 2
(TMQ 72008) Same above. Colored vinyl. 2 LP USA
HOT AS WELL
(White Knight WK 275) Deluxe brown & red cover. A copy of "Make Believe Ballroom" (TARKL 2979) minus 'The music never stopped' at the end of side 1. 2 LP USA
INTERVIEW WITH JERRY GARCIA
(Baktabak) Interview with Jerry. 1 LP EEC
IN TROUBLE CITY
(Dope Records 2) Miami Dec. 8, 1969. Pressed in blue vinyl, 1000 copies made. 1 LP EEC
JAMAICA
(Amazing Stork Rec. ASR 7485) Jamaican World Music Fest. Nov. 26, 1982. 2 LP USA
JOINT ADVENTURES
Akron Rubber Bowl July 2nd, 1986 w/Bob Dylan & Tom Petty. Deluxe box with booklet. 5 LP EEC
LIVE
Deluxe red & range cover. 2 LP USA
LIVE
(TMOQ 72014) Fold out color cover. Same as "Fillmore West" . 2 LP EEC
LIVE
(Berkeley 101) Same as "Felt Forum 1971". With insert. 1 LP USA
LIVE
(Record Revolution) Same above. 2 LP USA
LIVE AT FELT FORUM 1971
3 LP EEC
LIVE AT FELT FORUM
Same as "Felt Forum 1971". Picture disc released in 1979. 1 LP USA
LIVE AT FELT FORUM
(Impossible Record Works IMP 8101) Re-release of "Felt Forum 1971". 1 LP USA
LIVE AT FELT FORUM 1973
(Berkeley 2030) New York City 1973.

Available as "Rock & Roll Jamboree". With N.R.P.S.
2 LP USA
LIVE DEAD (Dittolino)
Same as "Fillmore West". 2 LP USA
LIVE FROM LONG BEACH, CA
(Tricky Dick Prod. ATDP 0849) Same as "The rose".
2 LP USA
LIVE IN CONCERT
(TMOQ 71037) FM broadcast. Fillmore West, San
Francisco Aug. 1971. 1 LP USA
LIVE IN CONCERT
(Mammary Productions MM 4) Same above. 1 LP
USA
LIVE IN CONCERT
(Mel 77) Same above. Red, white & blue picture
disc. 2000 copies made. 1 LP USA
LIVE IN CONCERT
(Mother Records) Same above. 1 LP USA
LIVE IN CONCERT
(S 2644 A/S 2645 B) Same above. 1 LP USA
LIVE IN COPENHAGEN VOL 1-2-3-4
(GD 001/2/3/4) Green vinyl. Copenhagen Oct. 8,
1981. 4 LP EEC
LIVE IN GIZAH, EGYPT
(Amazing Kornifone Rec. 1/2/3) Gizah, Egypt Sept.
14/15/16, 1978. Lim. ed. 500 copies with poster
and booklet. 3 LP EEC
LIVE IN GIZAH, EGYPT
(Deadcity Rec.) Same above. 500 nc. poster/
booklet. 3 LP EEC
LIVE IN MILWAUKEE
(Magic Bus Records 739) 1 LP USA
LIVE '69 & '70
Also available as "Central Park, Fillmore East,
Action House". 1 LP USA
LIVE IN PORTLAND, OREGON
(GDLC 001) Portland, Oct. 2, 1977. Limited
pressing of 280 copies. Deluxe b/w cover. 1 LP
USA
LIVE IN WESEL - 1 LP EEC
LIVING ON THE EDGE
(328) California 1968. Deluxe blue cover.
2 LP USA

LUNT FONTANE THEATRE
(Parrot Records) Jerry Garcia Band. New York, Oct.
15th, 1987. First Garcia's show after the coma.
1 LP USA
MADE MYSTIC HAMMERING
(Black & White Records) Eugene, Oregon July 19th,
1987. W/Bob Dylan. 2 LP USA
MAKE BELIEVE BALLROOM
(TAKRL 2979) Great American Music Hall, San
Francisco, Aug. 13rd, 1975. With insert. 2 LP USA
MAKE BELIEVE BALLROOM
(TAKRL 2929) Same above. Re-released in 1978
with a deluxe b/w cover. 2 LP USA
MAKE BELIEVE BALLROOM
(Ball 1/2/3/4 TAKRL 2979) Insert. Same above.
Copy of "Make believe Ballroom" (TARKL 2979). 2
LP USA
MAKE BELIEVE BALLROOM
(Beacon Island 2S 723) Same above. Deluxe colour
cover. 2 LP USA
MINESOTA BACKTRACKS
(Wizardo) 1 LP USA
MOE'S PLACE
(Impossible Record Works 1-103) Capitol Th.
Passaic Mar. 24, 1978. 1 LP USA
MOON MADNESS
(WRMB 389) Cover has sides reversed. 1 LP USA
MORE COSMIK MESSAGES
(CSR 004) Stoney Brook, New York City, Oct. 30th,
1970 (second show). Deluxe red & blue cover.
Deluxe label. Two tracks by Hot Tuna & David
Bromberg (18/1/'86). 1 LP EEC
MORE FROM WATKINS GLEN
(Vega Records 1) W/Allman Bros. & Beach Boys.
Watkins Glen, July 28th, 1973 (Not fade away). 1
LP USA
MOUNTAINS OF THE MOON
(Big Bang Records YLEM 1) Aoxomoxoa outtakes/
45 versions/Warlocks demo. 1 LP USA
NEW YEARS WITH THE DEAD
(Starlight SL 87024) Oakland Coliseum, Dec. 31th,
1988. Deluxe gold cover.
1 LP USA

NIGHT OF THE LIVING DEAD
(Blinding Light Records) Live 1970. With insert.
1 LP USA
NIGHT OF THE LIVING DEAD
(Starlight Records SL 87012) Avalon Ballroom, Apr.
6th, 1969 + Outtake 1969. Deluxe b/w cover. 1 LP
USA
OF DARK STARS & LOVELIGHT
(Dope 1) Fillmore East, New York, Feb. 11, 1970.
Deluxe colour cover. 1 LP USA
ORPHEUM THEATRE, BOSTON MASS.
Boston, Dec. 2, 1977. Deluxe blue cover. Actually
this is a Garcia show, not Dead. 1 LP USA
PUTTAKES
(005 GPT) "Terrapin Station" outtakes. 1 LP USA
OUT WEST
(Berkeley 2020/21) Live 1971. Also available as
"Hollywood Palladium 2". 2 LP USA
OUT WEST
(Impossible Record Works 2020/2021) Same
above. Re-release with a deluxe red & white cover.
2 LP USA
OWSLEY'S OWLS
(FLAT 8226) San Francisco, July 18, 1976. With
insert. 1 LP USA
OWSLEY'S OWLS
Same above. 150 coloured copies. 1 LP EEC
PALAIS DE SEINE, 1974 VOL. 1
Paris, Sept. 20/22, 1974. Deluxe b/w cover with
red lettering. 2 LP USA
PALAIS DE SEINE, 1974 VOL. 2
Same above. Deluxe b/w cover with blue lettering.
2 LP USA
PALAIS DE SEINE - Same above. 4 LP EEC
PHONETIC PHILISTINE
(Pharting Pharoah 13159) Toronto, Canada, June
30, 1987 (Part One). Deluxe colour cover. 2 LP
USA
RAMPPENS REVENGE 1
(Poow Productions) Empire Pool, Wembley,
London, Apr. 8th, 1972 + San Francisco 1974 +
Cow Palace, San Francisco, March. 23th, 1974 +
Capitol, NJ, June 1976. 2 LP USA

REMEMBRANCE OF THE HIPPIES PAST
(K & S 047) A limited pressing on multicolored
vinyl of "San Francisco 1". 1 LP USA
ROCK'N'ROLL JAMBOREE
2 LP USA
ROSE
(BS 1001) Santa Monica 1981. 2 LP USA
SAN FRANCISCO 1
(TMOQ 71058) FM broadcast from Fillmore West,
San Francisco 1971. 1 LP USA
SAN FRANCISCO
(K & S Records) Same above. 100 copies on
multicolored vinyl. Yellow insert. 1 LP USA
SAN FRANCISCO/LIVE FALL 1974
Live 1974. 1 LP USA
SHALOM
Also available as "Live in concert". With insert. 1
LP USA
SHRINE AUDITORIUM VOL. 1
(Koinè Records V880804) Live at the Shrine
Auditorium, Jefferson At Royal, Los Angeles, Nov.
8/9/10/11, 1967. 2 LP EEC
SHRINE AUDITORIUM VOL. 2
(Koinè Records V881103) Same above. 1 LP EEC
SILENT DEAD
(TMOQ 73010) Harpur College, Bringhampton May
2nd, 1970. 1 LP USA
SILENT DEAD
(TMOQ 73010) Same above. Coloured vinyl. 1 LP
USA
SPACE
(TMQ BBQ 006) Meadowlands, July 4th, 1987.
Limited edition of 500 copies. 2 LP USA
SPRING TOUR 1971
Live 1971 with insert. 1 LP USA
STELLA BLUE
(Shogun 13070) Spectrum Philadelphia, April 8,
1985. Deluxe colour cover. 2 LP USA
SUGAREE
(Berkeley 2244) 1 LP USA
SUGAR MAGNOLIA
(Berkeley 2266) Also available as "Live in concert".
Picture disc. 1 LP USA

SUNDOWN AT THE UNION
W/Bob Dylan. 2 LP EEC
THE ACID TRIP
(Sound City Prod. EX 2 7690) W/Ken Kesey, 1967.
Limited edition 300 copies. 1 LP USA
THE DEAD NON STOP
(Shirley Records) New York City 1980. 2 LP USA
THE LIVE ADVENTURES OF DYLAN & GARCIA
(Swingin' Pig TSP 016) Fow Warfield Th., San
Francisco, Nov. 16th, 1980. With Garcia on five
tracks. 1 LP EEC
THE MUSIC NEVER STOPPED
Raceway Park, Englishtown, NJ, Sep. 3, 1977.
1 LP USA
THE WARLOCKS
(The Eleven Records 2525) Los Angeles, May 3rd,
1965. Deluxe pink & black cover. 1 LP USA
THE WARLOCKS 20th ANNIVERSARY
(Grand Records 001 Greek G 1485) Greek Theatre,
Berkeley, June 14th, 1985. Deluxe colored cover,
red & white back. 2 LP USA
TIME AND DEAD
1 LP EEC
TOUCH OF GRAY
(Pharting Pharoah 13164) Eugene, Oregon, 1987
(part two) w/Bob Dylan. Deluxe b/w cover. 2 LP
USA
TRIUMPH
W/Bob Dylan. 2 LP USA

TURN ON YOUR LOVELIGHT
(Berkeley 2222) Live 1971. 1 LP USA
25 YEARS ON THE ROAD
(G-9091) Live in Berlin, Oct. 20, 1990. 2 LP EEC
UNCLE JOHN'S BAND LIVE AT THE ORPHEUM
(Hull Records GD 1276) Jerry Garcia Band. Deluxe
blue & white cover.
Deluxe label. 1 LP USA
UNKNOWN? WELLKNOWN?
200 copies. 1 LP EEC
VV. AA. CALIFORNIA CHRISTMAS ALBUM
(Penguin Egg 6/7) San Francisco, July 5, 1969
(Turn on your lovelight). With Janis Joplin.
2 LP EEC
VV. AA. CALIFORNIA EASTER ALBUM
(Penguin Egg 9/10) Garcia & Sarah (Tangent 1963)
+ Pig Pen & P. Albin. 2 LP EEC
VV. AA. MONTEREY POP FESTIVAL
(Evil Records 001/7) June 18th, 1967 *(Viola Lee
Blues, Cold rain & snow)*. Box 7 LP EEC
VV. AA. MONTEREY POP FESTIVAL 1967
(Document Records DR 021/26) Same above.
Box 6 LP EEC
WAKE OF THE FLOOD
(GD 01) 1 LP USA
WARLOX
(Berkeley 2013) Live 1970. With insert. 1 LP EEC
WINDWOOD ANDERSEN THEATRE
1 LP EEC

BOOTLEGRAPHY (CD)

In alphabetical order

ACOUSTIC DAZE
(Scorpio SC 13-15-780) Harpur College, May 2nd, 1970. 1 CD USA
AOXOMOXOA OUTTAKES
(The Early Years 02 CD 335) Outtakes 1969 + Nov. 14, 1967 + Demo Nov. 3, 1965. 1 CD EEC
BAY AREA BOOGIE
(Rockin' Records GDW 02) Oakland, Oct. 9th, 1976 (not '78 as the cover says) + Berkeley, July 13, 1984 + Oakland, Dec. 28th, 1982 + San Diego, Jan. 10, 1970. Deluxe color cardboard envelope. 1 CD USA
BETTER OFF DEAD
Live in '88. 1 CD EEC
BLOWING A RAINBOW
(PM-33185A) Portland, Maine March. 31st, 1985
COSMIC DEATH
(Flashback 125) Madison, Feb. 15, 1973. 1 CD EEC
COUPLA' SHOTS OF WHISKY
(Howdy Records CD 555-16) New York City, 1980. 1 CD USA
DEAD IN CORNELL PART 1-3
Live at Cornell University, Ithaca, May 8, 1977. 3 CD EEC
DEAD DE LUXE
(Boy 1-9065 CD) Luxembourg 5/16/1972. 1 CD EEC
DEAD SESSION
(Manic Depression MD 020) Live at Fillmore East, April 26, 1971 w/Duane Allman. 1 CD EEC
FOR DEAD HEADS ONLY
(Living Legend Records 016) Live 1968. 1 CD EEC
FRANKLIN'S TOWER
(Flashback 131) San Francisco August 13th, 1975. 1 CD EEC

GO AHEAD WITH A DEAD
Bob Dylan & Jerry Garcia, November 16, 1980. Aka "Live adventures". 1 CD EEC
GRATEFUL DEAD
(Curcio) Live in Rochester, 1970. 1 CD EEC
GRATEFUL DEAD
(Turn Your Player On TYPO 02) Oakland, 1988. 1 CD EEC
GRATEFUL DEAD
Live at Greek Theatre, May 22, 1982. 1 CD EEC
GRATEFUL DEAD LIVE
(CDDV5521) March 1, 1969. 1 CD EEC
GREETINGS FROM THE LIVING DEAD
(Living Legend Records LLR CD 008) San Francisco, March 1966 + Los Angeles, Jan. 1966. Deluxe color insert. 1 CD EEC
GUITAR POWER
(Chapter One CO 25148) Fillmore East, Feb. 11th, 1970. 1 CD EEC
HOUSTON 1972
(Rarities and Few RFR 1012) Houston, Nov. 19th, 1972. Same as "Texas stiffs". 1 CD EEC
IN CONCERT
(Living Legend Records 071) . Winterland, Dec. 31, 1978 + Meadowsland Arena NJ, Apr. 16, 1983 + Angel's Camp CA, Aug. 22/23, 1987. Feat. S. Stills and C. Santana. 1 CD EEC
LIVE & ALIVE
(IMT 15) Houston 1988. 1 CD USA
LIVE AT NASSAU COLISEUM
(NC 330901/2) Live March 30, 1990. 2 CD Canada
LIVE IN LOS ANGELES VOL. 1
(Black Panther BPCD 008) same of Shrine Auditorium (Koiné K880804)
LIVE IN LOS ANGELES VOL. 2
(Black Panther BPCD 009) same of Shrine Auditorium (Koiné K881103)
LIVE USA FEATURING SUZANNE VEGA
(Imtrat 900.015) New York City, Sep. 24, 1988. USA
LITTLE RED ROOSTER
(Turn Your Player On TYPO 02) Oakland Coliseum, Dec. 12, 1988. 1 CD EEC

MY HEAD IS DEAD
(Genuine Pig TGP124) Cover says live at University of Rochester 9/13/'70 but there was not show that day. It is Dillon Gym, Princeton University, 4/17/'71. 1 CD EEC
NEW YEAR'S EVE 1987/88
(Beech Marten BM 042) Oakland Coliseum Dec. 31st., 1987. 1 CD EEC
NEW YEAR'S EVE 1987/88 VOL. II
(Buccaneer Records BUC 039) Oakland Coliseum, Dec. 31st, 1987. 1 CD EEC
NEW YEAR'S EVE '89
(Rockin' Records GDW 01) Oakland Coliseum, Dec. 31st, 1988. 1 CD USA
ON THE TOP OF THE WORLD
(Pyramid 057) Strand Lyceum, London 5/23/'72. 1 CD EEC
OUT OF AN EASTERN PLANE
(WPOCM 1190 DO63-2) Live 1970. Boston, not at the University on 11/21/'70 but at the Boston Hall 4/7/'71. 1 CD EEC
OUT OF YOUR SKULL
Buffalo, N. Y., May 9, 1977. 2 CD USA
PORTLAND, MAINE
(PM 33185) 1 CD USA
PSYCHEDELIC BUS
(Wild Bird Records WBR CD 891006/7) Fillmore West, San Francisco, March 1st, 1969. Picture. 2 CD USA
SHRINE AUDITORIUM VOL. 1
(Koinè Records K 880804) Los Angeles, Nov. 8/9/10/11, 1967. 1 CD EEC
SHRINE AUDITORIUM VOL. 2
(Koinè Records K 881103) Same above. 1 CD EEC
TEA FOR THE DEAD
(Aulica A 115) Stony Brook, Oct. 10th, 1970. 1 CD EEC
TEXAS STIFFS
(Rockin' Records GDW 03) Houston, Nov. 19th, 1972. Deluxe color cardboard envelope. 1 CD EEC
THANK YOU UNCLE BOBO
(WBR 9122/23/224) Winterland, San Francisco, 31st Dec. 1978. W/John Cipollina, Lee Oscar, Mat Kelly, Ken Kesey, Ken Babbs & Merry Pranksters. Deluxe box + full colour booklet. 3 CD EEC
TIMELESS BEAUTY
(Lost Rose 01) Live at Community Concourse, San Diego, Jan. 10th, 1970. Picture.1 CD EEC
VINTAGE DEAD/HISTORIC DEAD
(SNF 5004) This illegal CD was taken off the two MGM/Sunflower LPs. 2 CD Canada
VV. AA. ALL AMERICAN JAM I & II
6 CD USA
VV. AA. GLASTONBURY FAYRE FESTIVAL
(Buc 029/2). With booklet; *Dark star*. 2 CD EEC
VV. AA. MONTEREY POP FESTIVAL 1967
(Document Records DR 022) Fairgrounds, Monterey, Ca., June 18, 1967. 1 CD EEC
VV. AA. MONTEREY POP FESTIVAL 1967
(Evil CD 2004/1/2) Same above. *Viola Lee Blues, Cold rain and snow*. With booklet. 2 CD EEC

FILMS & VIDEOS

THE MERRY PRANKSTERS SEARCH FOR THE COOL PLACE - A movie made by the Pranksters themselves. Circa 1965
ACID TEST - Private video shot by the Merry Pranksters in the Acid Tests. Shot in 1965
SONS & DAUGHTERS - A documentary film on the Oakland Peace March in October 1965. The Dead wrote the soundtrack. 1967
GRATEFUL DEAD - Robert Nelson's home movie of the Dead. Filmed in 1967
THE HIPPIE TEMPTATION *(CBS News, 1967)* - Includes interview with the band and footage of the Dead playing *Dancin' in the Streets*
COLUMBIA STRIKE *(1968)* - Movie about student rebellion. Includes Grateful Dead from May 3, 1968 playing at the Student Center Terrace
PETULIA - A movie directed by Richard Lester. The Dead appears in small footage and plays *Viola Lee blues* live. Realized in 1968
A NIGHT AT FAMILY DOG - With Grateful Dead, Jefferson Airplane and Santana. 1968
CALIBRATION - Grateful Dead, Quicksilver Messenger Service. Broadcast on local TV
NEW YEAR'S EVE 1968/69 - TV broadcast from Winterland, San Francisco, Dec. 31st, 1968
WOODSTOCK OUTTAKES (1969) - *High Time*
SAN FRANCISCO 1969 - Private video. B/W 13'.
PLAYBOY AFTER DARK
New York: TV show, July 10, 1969
NEW YEAR'S EVE 1969/70
TV broadcast from Winterland. First set only
NEW YEAR'S EVE 1970 - Only the first set broadcast on KQED
CELEBRATION *(1970)* - Grateful Dead and Quicksilver M. S. recorded at the KQED Studios in San Francisco on Aug. 30, 1970. Broadcasted by a local TV

WINTERLAND ARENA, S.F. - October 4, 1970 show. TV broadcast
UNCLE JOHN'S CHILDREN - Rare footage of the Danish TV on San Francisco musical scene. Released in 1971/72
TIVOLI GARDENS - TV broadcast from Danish TV. Release date April 17, 1972. 80 min.
FILLMORE: THE LAST DAYS - Directed by Richard T. Heffron. Excellent documentary on the closing of the mythic place in San Francisco. Bill Graham put together the best of the San Francisco sound. The Dead play only *Casey Jones* and a guncotton edition of *Johnny B. Goode*. The concert were filmed from June 29 to July 4, 1971. The movie has been released in 1972
RIDING THAT TRAIN - Same above
FIELD TRIP - This movie is a reckoning of the trip of the famous "Bus". The story is narrated by Ken Kesey and Ken Babbs. Contains rare stills of Neal Cassady. Realized in 1972
BEAT CLUB - Video clip (recorded live) for German TV. The line-up includes Pig Pen. Broadcasted on April 21, 1972. 8 min.
SUNSHINE DAYDREAM - August 27th, 1972, 82 min. An unreleased movie, includes Merry Pranksters footage of Acid Tests and their bus trips with Neal Cassady
THE GRATEFUL DEAD MOVIE - The official movie by the Grateful Dead. The footage has been shot at the farewell concerts in 1974. Incredible the cartoon sequence that open the movie, excellent through and through about deadheads
ORPHEUM THEATRE
Private video. July 13, 1976. 50 min.
DRAKE UNIVERSITY
April 23rd, 1976. Private video
ROOSEVELT STADIUM
New Jersey, 1976. Private, 90 min.
SAN FRANCISCO, 1978 - Private video
TONY SNYDER SHOW, 1978 - TV broadcast, 14'
SOUND AND LIGHT THEATRE, GIZAH EGYPT, 1978 Private video. 60 min.
SATURDAY NIGHT LIVE

NBC Studios, N. Y., TV show of Nov. 11, 1978
CAPITOL THEATRE - Passaic, NJ, Nov. 24, 1978. Private video, 180 min.
WINTERLAND CLOSING NIGHT - New Year's Eve 1978/79. 250 min. TV broadcast. W/John Cipollina, L. Oscar, M. Kelly, Ken Kesey, Ken Babbs and the Merry Pranksters. Superb!!!
TONY SNYDER SHOW, 1979
PORTRAIT OF A LEGEND - Release date 1980. 30 min. Various interviews and films
SATURDAY NIGHT LIVE
NBC Studios, N. Y., TV show of April 5, 1980
DEAD AHEAD, 1980 - Grateful Dead footage from October 30/31, 1980 performances at Radio City Music Hall, NYC
RADIO CITY MUSIC HALL (1980) - Close circuit telecast to a few theatres of Oct. 31, 1980 show
DEAD AHEAD, 1980 - Outtakes. 33 min.
AN EVENING WITH THE GRATEFUL DEAD (1981) - Broadcast as a showtime cable special of October 1980 shows
TODAY SHOW (1981) - Gene Shaut interview Garcia on the March 21, 1981 show
ROCKPALAST - March 28th, 1981. German TV broadcast, Grughalle, Essen 180 min.
TOMORROW SHOW
With Tom Snyder interviewing on May 7, 1981
VIETNAM: A TELEVISION HISTORY
TV broadcast, music by Mickey Hart. 1981
LATE NIGHT WITH DAVID LETTERMAN - Garcia and Weir appear on the Apr. 13, 1982 broadcast
ABC NIGHTLINE - Garcia's interview during the US Festival on Sept. 5, 1982
BACKSTAGE PASS (1982) - A '82 syndicated show
HELL'S ANGELS - Garcia/Saunders Band performs at the Hells Angels "Pirates Party" on Sep. 5, 1973. Executive producers are J. Garcia and Clare Frost. Released in 1983. Contains an unreleased studio version of Jerry Garcia Band's Takes a lot to laugh
THE SOUND OF SAN FRANCISCO (1983) - By Greg Kihn. 60 min.
HAIGHT-ASHBURY REVISITED (1983)
ONE MORE SATURDAY NIGHT - By Franken &

Davis. Garcia overdubs the guitar solo
LIVE AT THE OAKLAND COLISEUM ON NEW YEAR'S EVE (1985) - Produced by M. Hart and directed by Lenn Dell'Amico. 51 min.
BRIDGE BENEFIT (1985) - With Garcia, Weir, R. Wasserman, N. Young
NEW YEAR'S EVE 1985/86
Oakland, CA. Private video, 120 min.
THE TWILIGHT ZONE - By Phil DeGuere. Music by Grateful Dead and friends. 1986
FARM AID 2 - Broadcast date 1986, 19 min.
BALTIMORE - Oct. 8th, 1986. Private video, 6 min.
CLOSET CLASSICS - A non-stop all-hit rock retrospective. Grateful Dead are present with Dark star. 1986
NEW YEAR'S EVE 1986/87
TV broadcast. With the Neville Brothers
ROBERT HUNTER (Relix Video, 1987) - Video of the song from the Liberty album
THE HEROES JOURNEY: THE WORLD OF JOSEPH CAMPBELL - Soundtrack includes Jerry Garcia, Mickey Hart and Brent Mydland. 1987
DAY OF THE DEAD (1987) - MTV special
(IT WAS) TWENTY YEARS AGO TODAY (1987) - PBS documentary of the Summer of Love, includes the Grateful Dead at the Human Be-In with Timothy Leary on stage
AMERICA'S CUP - Promo video for the yacht races, music by Mickey Hart, 1987
FURTHER! KEN KESEY'S AMERICAN DREAMS
Ken Kesey and the Acid Tests with Merry Pranksters and the Grateful Dead. Produced by Joan Staffa and Steve Talbot. Released in 1987, 60 min.
FURTHERMORE!
Outtakes from Further! 1987, 30 min.
THE MAKING OF TOUCH OF GRAY
Directed by Justine Kreutzmann. Official video released in 1987
TOUCH OF GRAY
Official video clip released in 1987
HELL IN A BUCKET
Official video clip released in 1987
SO FAR - Official release in video only. Great

suggestion footage shot in New Year's Eve 1985-86 and Veteran Auditorium 1986. Released in 1987

LATE NIGHT WITH DAVID LETTERMAN
Garcia and Weir, Sep. 17, 1987

CIVIC AUDITORIUM - Jan. 28th, 1987. Private video, 6 min.

WORLD MUSIC SCHOOL CONCERT
Feb. 15th, 1987. With Garcia, Hart, B. Olatunji, C. Santana. 120 min.

EAST RUTHERFORD MEADOWLANDS NJ
July 12th, 1987. Bob Dylan & Grateful Dead, 90 min. Private video. B/W

OAKLAND COLISEUM CA - July 29th, 1987. Bob Dylan & Grateful Dead, 83 min. Private video

RED ROCKS - Morrison Colorado, Aug. 11, 1987. Private video, 135 min.

WARFIELD THEATRE - San Francisco, Dec. 17th, 1987. With Garcia, Weir, J. Baez. 35 min.

NEW YEAR'S EVE 1987
Oakland. With Neville Brothers

DOMINOES: A ROCK'N'ROLL JOURNEY THROUGH THE 60's
By John Lawrence, 1988. The 60's capturated by extraordinary imagery and classic rock'n'roll. Grateful Dead are present with *Dark star*

THROWING STONES
Official video clip. Released in 1988

DEADHEAD TV - Show 1. Apr. 1988
DEADHEAD TV - Show 2. May 1988
DEADHEAD TV - Show 3. June 1988
DEADHEAD TV - Show 4. July 1988
DEADHEAD TV - Show 5. Aug. 1988
DEADHEAD TV - Show 6. Sep. 1988
DEADHEAD TV - Show 7. Oct. 1988
DEADHEAD TV - Show 8. Nov. 1988

BRIDGE BENEFIT 2
Oakland Coliseum Dec. 2, 1988. Bob Weir

TIMELESS VOICES - GYUTO TANTRIC MONKS *(Fairwind Productions, 1988)* - Also includes performance by Mickey Hart

CASEY KASEN'S ROCK'N'ROLL GOLDMINE - THE SAN FRANCISCO SOUND *(1989)*

NIGHTLINE - ABC NEWS *(1989)* - Jerry Garcia, Bob Weir and Los Lobos playing an acoustic *This land is your land*

FOOLISH HEART *(Arista, 1989)* - Official videoclip

A LATINO SESSION - THE CINEMAX SPECIALS *(1989)* - Garcia, Santana, L. Ronstadt and others

AN EVENING WITH THE GRATEFUL DEAD *(1989)* - Grateful Dead in film and video performance

SWEETWATER INN SHOW - With Garcia, Weir, Sammy Hagar. Feb. 24, 1989. Private video 180'

DEADHEAD TV - Show 9. Jan. 1989
DEADHEAD TV - Show 10. Mar. 1989
DEADHEAD TV - Show 11. Apr. 1989
DEADHEAD TV - Show 12. May 1989

MOUNTAIN VIEW - California 1989. Private, 100'

VIRGINIA - Private, 1989, 120 min.

DEADHEAD TV - Show 13. June 1989

SUMMER SOLSTICE - Shoreline Amphiteatre, June 21, 1989. TV broadcast, w/Clarence Clemmons

DEADHEAD TV - Show 14. July 1989

JFK STADIUM Philadelphia, July 7, 1989 - Private video, 22 min.

AIDS BENEFIT - Release date 1989, 60 min.

BUILT TO LAST
Official video clip. Released in 1989

THE PEACE TAPES VOL. 1 - A VIDEO GUIDE TO THE PEACE *(1989)* - Includes Bob Weir

BUFFALO *(1989)* - Private video, 160 min.

GREEK THEATRE
Berkeley, Aug. 18, 1989. Private, 208 min.

GREEK THEATRE
Berkeley, Aug. 19, 1989. Private, 66 min.

NASSAU COLISEUM
Jerry Garcia Band. Sept. 6, 1989

DEADHEAD TV - Show 15. Sep. 1989

HAMPTON - Oct. 8th, 1989. Private video, 120'

DAVID LETTERMAN SHOW - Oct. 13th, 1989. TV broadcast with Garcia and Weir, 10 min.

NBC TODAY SHOW
Garcia and Weir interviewed on Oct. 31, 1989

DEADHEAD TV - Show 16. Nov. 1989

THE ACID TEST *(Key-Z Productions, 1990)* - Film footage of the acid tests

WE CAN RUN *(1990)* - This video of the song from *Built to last* was put together by the Dead and the National Aubodon Society
WE CAN RUN - Official video clip. Released in 1990
A SEASON OF WHALES *(Fairwind Productions, 1990)* - Music by Mickey Hart and Kitaro
JUST A LITTLE LIGHT *(1990)* - Official video clip
NASSAU COLISEUM
March 28, 1990. Private Video, 91 min.
NASSAU COLISEUM - Private, NYC 1990, 200 min.
TRANSFORMATION OF MYTH THROUGH TIME
By Joseph Campbell. Music performed by Jerry Garcia, David Jenkins and Brent Mydland
DEADHEAD TV - Show 17 - July 1990
MADISON SQUARE GARDEN
NYC, Sep. 14, 15, 19, 20, 1990. Private, 400 min.
THE SAN FRANCISCO SOUND *(1990)* - Anthology with Grateful Dead, J. Joplin, S. Miller...
A MIDNIGHT IN TOWN - Bruce Horsnby's video clip featuring Jerry Garcia. Live, 1990
SPECTRUM PHILADELPHIA
Provate video, 1990, 120 min.
STOCKHOLM SWEDEN - 1990, 110 min.
GERMANY - 1990, 120 min.
PARIS - Oct. 27, 1990. Private video, 120 min.
WEMBLEY LONDON - 1990, 120 min.
DEADHEAD TV - Show 18 - Nov. 1990
HARTFORD - 1990, 150 min. Private
INSTANT RECALL - Interviews with Jerry Garcia, Ken Kesey, Ken Babbs, David Gans and Toni Brown. Broadcasted on Jan. 22, 1991
NEW YORK - March 22, 1991. Private video, 120'
DEADHEADS - AN AMERICAN SUBCULTURE Produced by the Institute of Popular American Culture and the University of North Carolina at Greensboro. April 1991
NBC NIGHTLY NEWS - Summer 1991
KRON HEADLINERS *(1991)* - Jerry Garcia, Alice Walker and Carlos Santana interviewed by Suzanne Shaw.
NASSAU COLISEUM - March 1991, 100 min.
CALIFORNIA SCREAMIN' VOL. 3
Video with other artists. Release date1991

IN CONCERT - Giant's Stadium, June 16/17, 1991 with interview to Garcia and Weir
GIANTS STADIUM - June 17, 1991. Private, 220'
SPECIAL WILD SHOW - July 4th, 191, NYC. Mickey Hart w/Planet Drum. Promoting new book
BERKELEY IN THE SIXTIES
Grateful Dead perform *Viola Lee blues*. July 1991
MADISON SQUARE GARDEN - Sep. 1991, 240 min.
BOSTON - Sep. 22, 1991. Private, 180 min.
BOBBY & THE MIDNITES *(1991)*
Official video featuring Bob Weir.
BILL GRAHAM BENEFIT
San Francisco, Nov. 3rd, 1991. With Grateful Dead, CSN & Y, Santana, Jackson Browne, Joe Satriani, John Fogerty, Neil Young, Aaron Neville
JERRY GARCIA BAND
New York City, Nov. 11, 1991
NASSAU COLISEUM
New York, March 1992, 180 min. Private video
GRATEFUL DEAD - Compilation, 120 min.
I LOVE YOU ALICE B. TOKLAS
Film with Peter Sellers
DEADHEADS
A tye dye movie by Brian O' Donnell. 60 min. 1992
THE TRILL IS GONE - Video from Garcia/Grisman CD, directed by Justin Kreutzmann

BOOKS/MAGAZINES/FANZINES

THE GRATEFUL DEAD: THE HISTORY OF A FOLK STORY
by Gordon Hall Gerould - The Folklore Society, London 1907 - England. Anthology of tales about grateful dead. It is still the only one in existence.

THE PSYCHEDELIC EXPERIENCE
by Tim Leary, Ralph Metzner and Richard Alpert - Citadel Press - USA. A manual based on the Tibetan Book of the Dead.

THE ELECTRIC KOOL-AID ACID TEST
by Tom Wolfe - Farar, Straus & Giroux, New York 1968 - USA. Published in Italy by Feltrinelli, 1970 (Acid Test al Rinfresko Elettrico).
It's the chronicle of the deeds by Ken Kesey and Merry Pranksters.

THE JEFFERSON AIRPLANE AND THE SAN FRANCISCO SOUND
by Ralph J. Gleason - Ballantine Books, New York 1969 - USA. The liveliest and interesting witness on the San Francisco music scene.
Contains a long and interesting interview with Jerry Garcia.

WE ARE THE PEOPLE OUR PARENTS WARNED US AGAINST
by Nicholas Von Hoffman - USA. A view on the Summer 1967.

VOICES FROM THE LOVE GENERATION
by Leonard Wolf - USA. Book of interviews.

COPTATION: THE STORY OF A RADIO STATION
by Susan Krieger - USA. An accademic thesis on KMPX/KSAN.

SCENES
by John Irwin - USA. Essay on the Hippy and Surfer movements.

RINGOLEVIO: A LIFE PLAYED FOR KEEPS
by Emmett Grogan - USA.

THE STONED APOCALYPSE
by Marco Vassi - USA.

INFORMED SOURCES
by Willard Bain - USA. A novel on the psychedelic movement.

BE NOT CONTENT
by Billy Craddock - USA. A novel on the psychedelic movement.

THE DEAD BOOK: A SOCIAL HISTORY OF THE GRATEFUL DEAD
by Hank Harrison - Link Books, New York, 1970 - USA. Contains a flexi record of the band doing Trips music to Neal Cassady's rap.

TRIPPER
by Jocelyn - Exposition Press 1972. A portrait of the psychedelic life.

ENGLAND '72: BOOK OF DEAD
(Tour Book) - Warner Bros. 1972 - UK.

GARCIA: A SIGNPOST TO NEW SPACE
The Rolling Stone interview by Charles Reich and Jann Wenner plus a Stoned Sunday Rap with Jerry, Charles and Mountain Girl. Straight Arrow Books, 1972 - USA.

GRATEFUL DEAD SONGBOOK VOL. 1
Ice Nine/Warner Bros. 1972 - USA. Music and lyrics of Workingman's Dead and American Beauty.

GARCIA SONGBOOK
Ice Nine/Warner Bros. 1972 - USA. Lyrics and music of Garcia's first solo album.

NEW RIDERS OF THE PURPLE SAGE
Ice Nine/Warner Bros. 1972 - USA. Music and lyrics of their first album.

KESEY GARAGE SALE
by Ken Kesey - Viking Compass, 1973 - USA.

TURN IT UP (I CAN'T HEAR THE WORDS)
by Bob Scarlin - Simon and Shuster, New York, 1973 - USA. Contains a chapter about Robert Hunter.

THE GRATEFUL DEAD SONGBOOK VOL. 2
Ice Nine/Warner Bros. 1976 - USA. Lyrics and music of Wake of the flood, Mars Hotel, Blues for Allah.

GRATEFUL DEAD ANTHOLOGY
Ice Nine/Warner Bros. 1979/USA. Contains songs from various albums.

AQUARIAN ODISSEY
by Don Snyder - The N. Y. Times Company, 1979 - USA. Photos about Hippy movement.
MOUSE AND KELLY
Delta/Dell Publishing Co., New York, 1979 - USA. A portfolio of their artwork.
RICK GRIFFIN
by Gordon Mc Clenand - Perigee Books/G.P. Putman's Sons, N. Y. 1980 - USA. A portfolio of his artwork.
GRATEFUL DEAD: 1965-1980 SINGING THANK YOU FOR A REAL GOOD TIME
Grateful Dead Productions 1980 - USA. 12 pages picture booklet.
THE DEAD BOOK
Vol. 2 of a trilogy by Hank Harrison - Celestial Arts, 1980 - USA.
SUMMER OF LOVE
by Gene Antony - Celestial Arts, 1980 - USA. A photo documentary on the Haight Ashbury scene.
FAR AWAY RADIOS
by Robert M. Petersen - Privately printed - USA.
THE MUSIC NEVER STOPPED
by Blair Jackson - Delilah Communications, 1983 - USA.
THE OFFICIAL BOOK OF DEADHEADS
by Paul Grushkin, Cynthia Basset, Jonas Grushkin - William Morrow & C., 1983 - USA. The best witness on the Deadheads phenomenon.
GRATEFUL DEAD CONCERT PROGRAM 1983/84
Grateful Dead Production, 1983 - USA. Contains a meticulous research on the history and on the tales on the "Grateful Dead".
GRATEFUL DEAD
by Giancarlo Radice - Fabbri, 1983 - Italy.
TRUCKIN' WITH THE GRATEFUL DEAD TO EGYPT
by Robert Nicholas - Moonbow Press, 1984 - USA. Chronicle of the Egypt trip.
THE GRATEFUL DEAD SONGLIST
by Alasdair Mc Donald - Private Press, 1985 - UK. Firstly acoustic, then electric, performance of all songs ever performed by the Dead until December 1984.

PLAYING IN THE BAND
by David Gans & Peter Simon - St. Martin Press, 1985 - USA.
THE HAIGHT ASHBURY: A HISTORY
by Charles Perry - First Vintage Books, 1985 - USA. The most important book on the Haight Ashbury.
SAN FRANCISCO NIGHTS: THE PSYCHEDELIC MUSIC TRIP 1965/1968
by Gene Sculatti and David Seay - Sidgwick and Jakson Limited, 1985 - USA
SAN FRANCISCO ROCK 1965/1985
by Jack Mc Donough - Chronicle Books, 1985 - USA. The illustrated history of San Francisco Rock Music.
GRATEFUL DEAD GUITAR SUPERSTAR SERIES
Ice Nine/Warner Bros. 1986 - USA. Includes Super Tab notations.
DEAD LYRICS
Private Press, 1986 - Germany.
GRATEFUL DEAD "GUITAR MADE EASY" - Ice Nine/Warner Bros. 1986 - USA. Anthology of lyrics and music.
STORMING HEAVEN: LSD & THE AMERICAN DREAM
by Jay Stevens - Atlantic Monthly Press, 1987 - USA. An essay on LSD. Reprinted in 1991 by ATR Enterprises - USA.
TOUCH OF GREY
Ice Nine/Warner Bros. 1987 - USA. Lyrics and music from this album.
GRATEFUL DEAD "IN THE DARK"
Ice Nine/Warner Bros. 1987 - USA. Lyrics and music of the same album.
THE ART OF ROCK
by Paul Grushkin - Abbeville Press, 1987 - USA. The masterpiece book on rock posters.
FLASHING ON THE SIXTIES
by Lisa Law - Chronicle Books, 1987 - USA. Photographs on the 60's.
DEAD BASE - THE COMPLETE GUIDE TO THE GRATEFUL DEAD SONGLISTS
by John W. Scott, Mike Dolguskin and Stu Nixon - Hanover NH, 1987 - USA. The best and amazing thing I ever saw about the Grateful Dead.

DEAD BASE II - THE COMPLETE GUIDE TO THE GRATEFUL DEAD SONGLISTS
by John W. Scott, Mike Dolguskin and Stu Nixon - Hanover NH, 1988 - USA.

ALLEYS OF THE HEART
by Robert M. Petersen - Hulogos'i Books, 1988 - USA. Collected poems by the Grateful Dead's lyricist Robert M. Petersen. Foreword by Robert Hunter.

DUINO ELEGIES
Hulogos'i Books, 1988 - USA. Robert Hunter's translation of Rilke's classic Duino Elegies, illustrated by Maureen Hunter.
Available also in a Joint paperback and Cassette Tape Edition, read by Robert Hunter, accompanied by Tom Constanten on piano.

DEAD TOUR
a novel by Alan Neal Izuni - Relix, 1988 - USA.

DEAD BASE '88 - THE ANNUAL EDITION OF THE COMPLETE GUIDE TO THE GRATEFUL DEAD SONGLISTS
by John W. Scott, Mike Dolguskin and Stu Nixon - Hanover NH, 1989 - USA.

DEAD BASE III - THE COMPLETE GUIDE TO THE GRATEFUL DEAD SONGLISTS
by John W. Scott, Mike Dolguskin and Stu Nixon - Hanover NH, 1989 - USA.

GRATEFUL DEAD FAMILY ALBUM
by Jerilyn Lee Brandelius. Warner Bros. 1989, USA Superb with unpublished photos.

GRATEFUL DEAD FOLKTALES
by Bob Franzosa. Zosafarm Pub., 1989, USA.

WHAT A LONG STRANGE TRIP IT'S BEEN
by Lewis Saunders, 1989 - USA. A book about the Hippies.

THE WATER OF LIFE
by Alan Trist, Hulogos'i Books, 1989 - USA. A tale of the Grateful Dead.

BUILT TO LAST
Ice Nine/Warner Bros. 1990 - USA. Lyrics and music of the same album.

BOOK OF DEAD
by Herb Green - Delta, 1990 - USA.

Photographic book.

GRATEFUL DEAD SUPERTAB ANTHOLOGY FOR GUITAR - Warner Bros. 1990 - USA.
Anthology of lyrics and music.

GRATEFUL DEAD TWENTY FIVE YEARS
Grateful Dead Productions, 1990 - USA.
Tour program.

THE DEAD VOL. 2
by Hank Harrison - Archives Pr., 1990 - USA.

DRUMMING AT THE EDGE OF THE MAGIC
by Mickey Hart - Harper, 1990 - USA.

A BOX OF RAIN
by Robert Hunter - Viking, 1990 - USA.
Collected lyrics of Robert Hunter.

BUILT TO LAST "GRATEFUL DEAD 25th ANNIVERSARY"
by Jamie Jensen - Plume, 1990 - USA.

THE HISTORY OF THE GRATEFUL DEAD
by William Ruhlmann - Gallery, 1990 - USA.

PSYCHEDELIA: THE CLASSICAL POSTER BOOK
Octopus Book Limited, 1990 - USA.
Portfolio with 6 psychedelic posters.

THE DEAD VOL. 1
by Hank Harrison - Archives, 1990 - USA.
Formerly "The Dead Book" - revisited 1990.

FURTHER by Ken Kesey - Viking, 1990 - USA.
A finction story based on the trip of 1965 of the Merry Pranksters.

ON THE BUS
by Ken Babbs, Thunder's Mouth Press, 1990 - USA.
A celebration of the unforgettable exploits of the Merry Pranksters. Foreword by Hunter S. Thompson and Jerry Garcia.

GRATEFUL DEAD SONG LYRICS
Private Press, 1990 - USA.

DEAD BASE '89 - THE ANNUAL EDITION OF THE COMPLETE GUIDE TO THE GRATEFUL DEAD SONGLISTS
by John W. Scott, Mike Dolguskin and Stu Nixon - Hanover NH, 1990 - USA.

DEAD BASE IV - THE COMPLETE GUIDE TO THE GRATEFUL DEAD SONGLISTS
by John W. Scott, Mike Dolguskin and Stu Nixon -

Hanover NH, 1990 - USA.
NIGHT CADRE
by Robert Hunter - Viking Penguin, 1991 - USA
ONE MORE SATURDAY NIGHT
by Sandy Troy - St. Martin's, 1991 - USA.
CONVERSATIONS WITH THE GRATEFUL DEAD
by David Gans - Citadel, 1991 - USA.
The Grateful Dead interview book.
SUNSHINE DAYDREAMS "A GRATEFUL DEAD
JOURNAL" by Herb Green - Chronicle, 1991 - USA.
PLANET DRUM: A CELEBRATION OF PERCUSSION
AND RHYTM by Federic Liebman & Mickey Hart
Harper Collins, 1991 - USA.
PANTHER DREAM
by Bob and Wendy Weir - 1991 - USA. A Book-Tape
set about life in the african rainforest.
GRATEFUL DEAD, AESTHETICS OF THE
by D. Womak - 1991 - USA. Limited edition.
Musical analysis.
GRATEFUL DEAD
by Massimo Cotto and Pasquale Di Bello - Arcana
Editrice, 1991 - Italy.
DEAD BASE '90 - THE ANNUAL EDITION OF THE
COMPLETE GUIDE TO THE GRATEFUL DEAD
SONGLISTS
by John W. Scott, Mike Dolguskin and Stu Nixon -
Hanover NH, 1991 - USA
DEAD BASE V - THE COMPLETE GUIDE TO THE
GRATEFUL DEAD SONGLISTS
by John W. Scott, Mike Dolguskin and Stu Nixon -
Hanover NH, 1991 - USA
GRATEFUL DEAD: SELECTION FROM AMERICAN
BEAUTY - Classic Supertab, 1991 - USA.
Lyrics and music from this album.
GRATEFUL DEAD: SELECTION FROM
WORKINGMAN'S DEAD
Classic Supertab, 1991 - USA.
Lyrics and music from this album.
GRATEFUL DEAD WITHOUT A NET
Classic Supertab, 1991 - USA.
Lyrics and music from this album.
GRATEFUL DEAD THE BEST OF
USA. Anthology of lyrics and music for guitar.

GRATEFUL DEAD ANTHOLOGY FOR GUITAR
Ice Nine/Warner Bros. - USA. Anthology of lyrics
and music. Arranged by Mark Phillips.
GRATEFUL DEAD THE BEST OF
USA. Anthology for piano, voice and guitar.
BETWEEN ROCK AND HARD PLACES
by Tom Constanten - USA. Tom Constanten's
autobiography. 1992
THE PSYCHEDELIC YEARS - Music, dreams &
Colours San Francisco 1965/1969. Book, cards &
live CD. Stampa Alternativa, Italy, 1992
SOUND SYSTEM ENGINEERING
by Don & Carolyn Davis - Essay on Grateful Dead's
"Wall of sound" in 1974.
GRATEFUL DEAD: THE UNAUTHORIZED
BIOGRAPHY IN COMICBOOK
Revolution Comics, 1992 - USA. #45 The early
years; #46 The seventies; #47 Through today.
AGES BACK TO BACK
by Scott Allen - Aces Inc., 1992 - USA.
DARK STAR MAGAZINE
An excellent english magazine from the seventies.
Out of print.
RELIX
P. O. Box 94, Brooklyn, New York, 11229 USA. A
magazine almost entirely dedicated to Grateful
Dead. Excellent.
THE GOLDEN ROAD
484 Lake Park Ave., Oakland, CA 94610 USA.
Magazine. Edited by Blair Jackson. Rich in news by
the band and made in excellent way.
SHINE INSIDE
Loodsdon Drive, Anandle VA 22003 USA.
Newsletter by Rob & Carol Bruce.
SPIRAL LIGHT
English fanzine c/o Rob and Maggie Kedward, 121
Park Palace, Amersham Bucks HP6 6NP - U.K.
DEAD BASE: THE COMPLETE GUIDE TO GRATEFUL
DEAD SONGLISTS 1965/1990
P. O. Box 499, Hanover, NH 03755 USA.
It's a must!
DEAD BEAT
Newsletter c/o The Grateful Dead Historical Society,

Box 1188 Amherst, Mass. 01004 USA.
THE MUSIC NEVER STOPS
English fanzine about Grateful Dead and Hawkwind.
Not available now, c/o Alasdair Mc Donald, Wildfield
House, Clenchwarton, King's Lynn - U.K.
DEAD HEAD TV A
1/2 hour monthly news magazine show. Tour
reports, interviews with musicians and curent
news about Dead Heads. P. O. Box 170642, San
Francisco, CA 94117 - USA.
THE ARCHIVES PRESS
Grateful Dead newsletter. 1259 El Camino Real
#188, Menlo Park, CA 94025 - USA.
RIPPLE
An Italian fanzine on the Grateful Dead. Only two
issues published, each with a freebie single by the
Dead. Entirely written in English, with Italian
translation. Next issue will be available on (dream)
Summer 1993.
Fanzine italiana sui Grateful Dead. Attualmente

due numeri all'attivo, entrambi con un singolo dei
Dead in omaggio. Scritta completamente in ingle-
se con traduzione italiana allegata. Prossimo nu-
mero Estate 1993.
c/o Pasquale Di Bello - Via Bronzino, 29 - 50142
Firenze - Italy.
UNBROKEN CHAIN
American fanzine about the Grateful Dead. P. O.
Box 8726 - Richmond, VA 23226 - USA.
DUPREE'S DIAMOND NEWS
Superb magazine documenting the Dead Head
experience. P. O. Box 3603, N.Y., NY 10185 - USA.
GRATEFUL DEAD COMIX
Kitchen Sink Press, N. 2 Swamp Rd., Princeton WI
54968 - USA.
GRATEFUL DEAD
Deadtime stories. Masters of Rock, P. O. Box 410,
Mt. Morris, IL 61054 - USA.
GENERAL INFORMATIONS DEAD HEADS
P. O. Box 1065, San Rafael, Ca. - USA

JOY DIVISION
with 7" Lit. 14.000/with mini-CD Lit. 16.000
MARC ALMOND AND THE SOFT CELL
with 7" Lit. 14.000/with mini-CD Lit. 16.000
ROBERT WYATT *with 7" Lit. 13.000*
SYD BARRETT
with 7" Lit. 14.000/with mini-CD 16.000
SISTERS OF MERCY
with 7" Lit. 14.000/with mini-CD Lit. 16.000
COAST TO COAST PUNK ROCK IMAGES
with 7" Lit. 13.000
VELVET UNDERGROUND
with 7" Lit. 14.000/with mini-CD Lit. 16.000
PAUL ROLAND *with 7" Lit. 14.000*
THE RESIDENTS *with 7" Lit. 15.000*
BILLY BRAGG *with 7" Lit. 14.000*
CCCP *with 7" Lit. 16.000*
BAUHAUS *with 7" Lit. 15.000*
JOY DIVISION: From the centre of the city
with 7" Lit. 15.000/with mini-CD Lit. 17.000
GENESIS P-ORRIDGE/PSYCHIC TV
with mini-CD Lit. 18.000
HIP HOP RAP Word power *with 7" Lit. 15.000*
HAWKWIND
The never ending story of the psychedelic warlords
with 30' live CD Lit. 18.000
SONIC YOUTH *with 7" Lit. 16.000*
THE JESUS AND MARY CHAIN
with mini-CD Lit. 18.000
THE PSYCHEDELIC YEARS
with 20 colour postcards and a live CD
(Grateful Dead, Jefferson Airplane,
Quicksilver Messenger Service) Lit. 20.000
GRATEFUL DEAD *with 60' live CD Lit. 20.000*

All the books
are written in English
and Italian
and contains lyrics,
biographies and
discographies
of the artists
The prices are
in Italian Liras

**Redazione
Editorial Office:**

STAMPA
ALTERNATIVA
P.O. Box 741
00100 ROMA

**Magazzino
Warehouse:**

NUOVI
EQUILIBRI
P.O.Box 97
01100 VITERBO
Fax 0761/352751

**Distribuzione
ufficiale
Official distributor:**

MATERIALI SONORI
Via Trieste, 35
52027 SAN GIOVANNI
VALDARNO (Ar)
Fax 055/9120370

SCONCERTO